Principles of Bookkeeping Controls

Tutorial

David Cox
Michael Fardon

Published by Osborne Books Limited
Tel 01905 748071
Email books@osbornebooks.co.uk
Website www.osbornebooks.co.uk

Design by Laura Ingham

Printed by CPI Group (UK) Limited, Croydon, CR0 4YY, on environmentally friendly, acid-free paper from managed forests.

British Library Cataloguing in Publication Data
A catalogue record for this book is available from the British Library

ISBN 978-1-911198-52-9

Contents

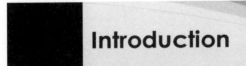

Introduction

Qualifications covered

This book has been written specifically to cover the Unit 'Principles of Bookkeeping Controls' which is mandatory for the following qualifications:

AAT Level 2 Certificate in Accounting

AAT Level 2 Certificate in Bookkeeping

AAT Certificate in Accounting – SCQF Level 6

The book contains a clear text with worked examples and case studies, chapter summaries and key terms to help with revision. Each chapter concludes with a wide range of activities, many in the style of AAT computer based assessments.

Osborne Study and Revision Materials

Additional materials, tailored to the needs of students studying this unit and revising for the assessment, include:

- **Workbooks:** paperback books with practice activities and exams
- **Wise Guides:** pocket-sized spiral bound revision cards
- **Student Zone:** access to Osborne Books online resources
- **Osborne Books App:** Osborne Books ebooks for mobiles and tablets

Visit www.osbornebooks.co.uk for details of study and revision resources and access to online material.

1 Payment methods

this chapter covers...

This chapter is an introduction to the payment methods of UK banks and other financial providers to individuals and businesses. It describes the following payment methods:

- *cash*

- *cheques*

- *debit cards (including 'tap and go' cards)*

- *credit cards*

- *bank drafts*

- *electronic bank transfers (BACS, standing orders, direct debits, Faster Payments, CHAPS)*

This chapter explains how these different payment methods work and how they are suitable for different circumstances.

METHODS OF PAYMENT – AN INTRODUCTION

There are a number of different methods of payment used by individuals. Developments in technology over recent years have resulted in changes in the ways in which payments are made, for example:

The **increased** use of:

- plastic cards – debit cards, credit cards

- electronic payments between bank accounts – BACS, direct debits, standing orders, Faster Payments

- electronic devices such as computers, tablets, smart phones and some smart watches, which can be set up with the user's debit or credit card details to make mobile payments

A **decline** in the use of:

- cash

- cheques

In the first part of this chapter we will describe both the traditional ways of making payments – cash and cheques – and also the more recent developments in making payments electronically – BACS, direct debits, standing orders, Faster Payments.

CASH

Cash remains one of the simplest methods of making payment for goods and services, particularly where small amounts are involved. Some businesses – shops, for example – take cash (ie notes and coins) in payment for goods and services. This is paid into the bank on a regular basis; if it were left on the business premises it would pose a security risk.

The use of cash for making small payments is declining with widespread use of 'tap and go' debit and credit cards, and payment systems linked to smart phones and watches.

Cash is still used by a business as a payment method for **cash wages** (although this is rare nowadays) and also for a **petty cash** system. As you will know from your studies of bookkeeping transactions, petty cash is a limited amount of cash kept within the business to make small incidental expense payments, eg stationery or postage stamps. This petty cash will need topping up from time to time with cash withdrawn from the bank account of the business.

CHEQUES

Payment by cheque was at one time in common use by businesses and individuals, but is now declining rapidly. Some large retail stores refuse to accept them. Cheques are still used for payments made by post, eg payment of bills and payment by business customers settling up a supplier account, although, increasingly, other methods are available.

what is a cheque?

A cheque is an instruction in writing, signed by the bank's customer (who is paying the money) telling the bank to pay an amount to a named person or business (who is receiving the money).

If you receive a cheque you will often have to pay it into an account at a bank or building society, although cheques can be 'paid in' electronically using a bank's app on a mobile phone to photograph the cheque.

Great care must be taken both when writing out a cheque and also when receiving cheques in payment; they must be checked to ensure that all the details are correct. If they are not correct, the cheque may be invalid and it may not be paid by the payer's bank and the money amount taken from your account.

In short, cheques are not only time consuming to process, they also carry the risk that they will not be paid by the bank and you will lose your money if they 'bounce'. A specimen cheque is shown below.

the people involved in a cheque

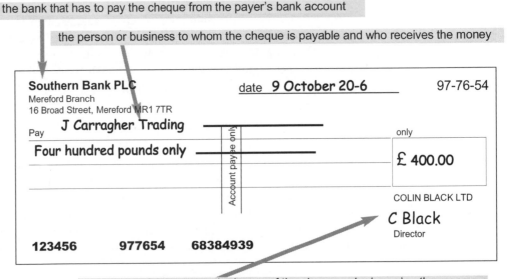

issuing of cheques

When writing out a cheque (using ink, not pencil), care should be taken to complete the following details:

- the correct date

- the name of the person or business receiving the money (the payee)

- the amount in words (except the pence which can be in numbers)

- the amount in figures (which should be the same as the amount in words)

- authorised signature (it may be that of a supervisor or director)

- counterfoil (date, amount, payee)

No room should be left on the cheque for possible fraudulent additions or alterations; any blank spaces should be ruled through with a single line.

If any errors are made when writing out the cheque, they should be corrected and the authorised signature placed close to the alteration in order to tell the bank that it is an approved correction.

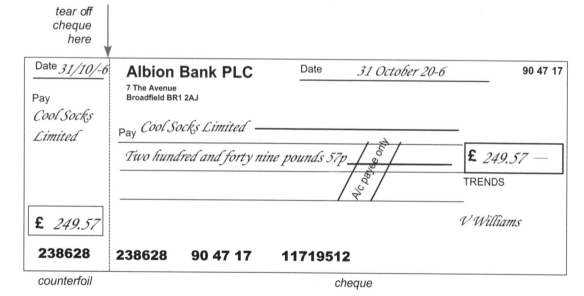

counterfoil　　　　　　　　　　　　　　　　　　　*cheque*

PAYMENT BY PLASTIC CARD

There are a number of types of plastic cards commonly used as a means of payment. They include:

- **debit cards** – where payment is taken from the bank account of the customer

■ **credit cards** – where monthly payment is made in full or in part by the customer

The electronic methods used to process the payments for these cards include:

■ 'Chip and PIN' technology where the cardholder slides the card into the terminal and enters a PIN (Personal Identification Number)

■ 'tap and go' where the card details are transferred to the terminal by 'tapping' or swiping the card on the terminal – there are money amount limits for such transactions

■ a terminal or web link where the customer is not present and the transaction is a mail order, telephone or online purchase, processed remotely using the card details provided by the cardholder

debit cards

Debit cards enable the card holders to make payments from their bank accounts electronically when they make purchases.

Debit card issuers include Visa and Mastercard. The money is reserved immediately and is normally taken from the bank account the day after purchase, but can take longer.

Provided that there is sufficient money in the card holder's bank account (or an arranged overdraft facility), debit card payments can be for any amount. Larger payments may need to be verified with answers to security questions.

credit cards

Credit cards are a means of buying goods and services immediately and for withdrawing cash from ATMs. Credit cards are also used for mail order, telephone and online purchases.

Sellers of goods and services use a **card merchant** to process their card payments, and pay a set percentage (up to 5%) of each transaction amount for the use of the credit card facility.

Each month the cardholder receives a paper or online statement of the purchases made in the previous month and can choose to pay off the full balance of the account, or to pay part only, carrying forward the remaining balance to next month.

Payment is commonly made by direct debit or debit card. Interest is charged on any balance still owing to the credit card company after the monthly payment date. Some cards charge an annual flat fee to the cardholder for the use of the card.

Credit cards are issued with credit limits for the maximum amount that can be owing on the card at any one time. The credit limits cannot be exceeded.

ELECTRONIC BANK TRANSFERS

BACS system

Bankers Automated Clearing Services (BACS) is a computer electronic transfer payment system owned by Bacs Payment Schemes Limited. It is used by banks for regular payments such as insurance premiums, payment of trade debts, wages and salaries. BACS is a cheap and efficient means of payment because, instead of a piece of paper (eg a cheque) having to be prepared and sent off, the transfer is set up on a computer file and transferred between the banks' computers – the payment goes direct from account to account after three working days.

BACS direct credits

Businesses often need to make regular payments of **variable** amounts, eg:

- paying wages and salaries

- making payments to suppliers at the end of each month

The BACS **direct credit** system is used to process such variable payments. Whenever payments are due to be paid, the business sends a schedule electronically to its bank, setting out the details of the payments. **The payment cycle is three working days.** This means that, if a business wants its suppliers or employees to have the money in their accounts on Friday, the instruction to pay the money must be made on Wednesday.

Faster Payments

Faster Payments are same-day electronic bank transfer payments from one account to another account at a bank or building society. Features are:

- customer instructions for payment may be given to the bank by telephone and online banking

- customer instructions include the name of the account to receive the payment, account number, sort code and an identifying reference number

- the customer must have enough money in the account for the payment

- the payment will be received almost immediately, but could take up to **two hours** to reach its destination account; once the payment has been sent it cannot be cancelled

- the bank sending the payment will receive an acknowledgement that the payment has been made when it reaches its destination account; if there is a problem with the payment at the receiving bank, it will be rejected and the sending bank will be notified

- Faster Payments are used for making **standing order** payments

standing orders

Standing orders are used to make regular payments of the same amount, eg a loan repayment, rent payment. The bank customer gives authority to the bank, along with details of what payments to make, to whom, and when. This authority can be given in writing or online. The bank then sets up the instructions on its computer and the payments are made automatically by computer, usually using **Faster Payments**.

BACS direct debits

The direct debit system is used by businesses such as insurance companies that are due a large number of variable amount receipts:

- direct debits can be used for fixed and variable amounts and/or where the time intervals between payments vary

- the business that receives payment prepares the computer instructions requesting the payer's bank account for payment using the banking system

As with BACS direct credits, the BACS direct debit payment time is **three working days**. For example, if payment is to be made on a Friday, the instructions for the transfer must be made on Wednesday to the bank computer systems. The money is then transferred from account to account three days later, on the Friday.

mobile electronic payments

A current development in payment technology is the establishment of a database which allows owners of smart phones to make mobile electronic payments from their bank or credit card to another person or business.

Payments can be made as follows:

- download an app from the bank or credit card provider

- enter a PIN number or password to log on to the app

- choose the recipient (who must also have an app downloaded from their bank or credit card provider) and select the recipient's mobile phone number

- enter an amount to pay, and confirm the payment transaction

The payment will then be made as a Faster Payments transfer.

'ONE-OFF' LARGE PAYMENTS

Individuals and businesses can make 'one-off' large payments using the bank CHAPS system or by issuing bank drafts.

CHAPS

CHAPS (Clearing House Automated Payments System) is used for high value same-day payments made by electronic bank transfer. A common use of CHAPS is when solicitors are arranging the transfer of funds for the purchase and sale of property on behalf of clients. CHAPS payments cannot be cancelled after they have been sent. There is no minimum or maximum payment limit.

bank drafts

A person or business may have to make a large purchase and be asked to pay by bank draft. A bank draft is a document like a cheque written out by a bank and the purchaser pays the bank (plus a charge) from the purchaser's bank account. In this way the purchaser gets the bank to issue a paper-based payment that cannot be stopped or 'bounced' (returned unpaid). It is therefore a very secure way of making payment. There is no minimum or maximum payment limit.

Case Study

CHOOSING THE RIGHT METHOD OF PAYMENT

situation

Shamina Jiwa works as a manager in the accounts department of Helicon Limited. She authorises payments for company expenses.

In her in-tray are the following payments or payment requests that need to be dealt with. What methods of payment would you expect her to use or recommend in each case? How long will it take for the payment to reach each destination?

1   A top-up of the department's petty cash float. It needs £78.60 to bring it up to the £100 limit.

2   £120,000 for new delivery vans. The dealer has asked for 'the next best thing to cash', preferably a paper-based payment.

3   A £500 charity donation to Cancer UK which needs to be posted together with a personal letter from the Managing Director.

4   A new supplier who wants prompt payment at the end of every month. The statement totals will vary between approximately £450 and £150.

5   Loan repayments to a finance company for a fixed amount of £395 a month.

6 The deposit for a new office building: £150,000 is required by a firm of solicitors to be paid to their account this afternoon.

7 A newly-appointed sales manager needs a means of payment for settling her travel and hotel expenses.

8 A 'one-off' payment of £550 for office furniture – it is a special offer and payment has to be made to the seller by the end of the day.

suggested solutions

Shamina is likely to use or recommend the following payment methods:

1 The petty cash top-up of £78.60 will need to be withdrawn as cash from the bank using a cheque by an employee of Helicon Ltd. The transaction is same day.

2 The 'next best thing to cash' for a £120,000 payment for delivery vans is likely to be a bank draft which will be handed to the dealer on the purchase date.

3 A £500 donation posted to a charity will best be made by sending a cheque, which makes the transaction more 'personal'. The timescale will depend on the speed of the postal service.

4 A new supplier who is to be paid variable amounts at the end of every month could be paid electronically by BACS direct credit, which is ideal for variable amounts. This payment will arrive three working days after giving instructions to the bank.

5 Loan repayments to a finance company for a fixed amount of £395 a month would ideally be made by setting up a standing order using the Faster Payments system. Payment will be same day.

6 The deposit of £150,000 for a new office building is required on the same day and is a large amount, so a CHAPS electronic transfer is likely to be used.

7 The sales manager who needs to pay for her business expenses is most likely to use a business credit card. The timescale here is based on the monthly payment date for the card.

8 An urgent same-day payment of £550 for office furniture is likely to be made using the Faster Payments service. Payment will take up to two hours.

Chapter Summary

■ The current trend in payment methods is a marked increase in the use of electronic payments and a decline in the use of paper-based payments such as cheques.

■ Cash has for a long time been the traditional form of payment for small value transactions. Businesses sometimes use cash for the payment of wages; it is also needed for the petty cash system.

■ Cheques are still used in business for postal payments, for example the settling of supplier accounts, but a cheque carries the risk to the payee that it might be returned unpaid (ie it may 'bounce').

■ Debit cards are commonly used for making purchases. The amount of the purchase is normally taken from the bank account the day after the purchase.

■ Credit cards are used to make purchases and payment will normally be made in full or in part a month later on receipt of a statement.

■ The BACS system is used for making direct payments between bank accounts by direct debit and direct credit. The clearance cycle is three working days (the money passes from account to account on the third day).

■ Faster Payments is a same-day two hour maximum computer payment service used by the banks for standing orders, telephone and online payments.

■ Same-day payments for large of amounts of money can be made by CHAPS (a computer-based bank transfer system) or by bank draft (a bank paper document, which looks like a cheque, issued by the bank).

Key Terms		
	cheque	a cheque is an instruction in writing, signed by the bank's customer (who is paying the money), telling the bank to pay an amount to a named person or business
	debit card	a card which can be used for purchases and cash withdrawals; payment is normally taken from the bank account on the next working day
	credit card	a card issued on a 'buy now and pay later' basis and for cash withdrawals; payment is made monthly in full or in part on receipt of a statement
	electronic bank transfer	a term used to describe the electronic transfer of funds through the banks' computer systems
	BACS	Bankers Automated Clearing Services – a system used by banks to make computer-based direct payments between bank accounts
	BACS direct credits	direct BACS payments between bank accounts – with a three day clearance (the transfer is made three working days after the instructions are given)
	standing order	regular (fixed date, same amount) payments, set up with the bank by the business sending the money
	direct debit	variable date and amount BACS payments, set up by the business receiving the payments through their bank
	Faster Payments	same-day payments (up to 2 hours) between banks – the instructions can be given at the bank branch, by telephone or online
	CHAPS	high value, same-day payments sent through the banks' computer systems (Clearing House Automated Payment System) – cannot be cancelled after they have been sent
	bank draft	a paper-based document (similar to a cheque) issued by a bank – as good as cash – used for high value purchases; cannot be stopped or cancelled after it has been issued

Activities

1.1 Cash is most likely to be used as a means of payment by a business in which **two** of the following situations. Tick the correct options.

(a)	Small items of office expenditure	
(b)	The wages of an employee who has a bank account	
(c)	The wages of an employee who does not have a bank account	

1.2 A cheque is:

(a)	A written and signed instruction by a customer to their bank to pay a specific amount of money to a named person or business	
(b)	A written and signed instruction to a named person or business stating that they will pay a specific amount of money by a specific date	
(c)	A written and signed instruction by a customer to their bank to pay a specific amount of money on a specific date to a named person or business	

Which **one** of these options is correct?

1.3 A debit card has the following features. Tick the 'true' or 'false' columns as appropriate.

		True	False
(a)	It allows a business to pay for a number of purchases in one amount at the end of each month		
(b)	It always requires a PIN number entered on a terminal when a payment is made		
(c)	It cannot be used to make payments online		
(d)	Payment is taken from the bank account of the card holder		

1.4   A credit card is a useful form of payment for a business because:

(a)	It is a secure way of making very large payments	
(b)	No interest is ever charged on the amount outstanding on the card	
(c)	It can be used for a sales representative who travels for the business and has to pay for expenses incurred	

Which **one** of these options is correct?

1.5   Standing orders are best suited for payments which:

(a)	Are equal in amount	
(b)	Are variable in amount	
(c)	Are made on different dates in the month	

Which **one** of these options is correct?

1.6   You are running a business and need to make various payments each month. Which method of payment from the list provided at the end of the question would you choose as the best to use in the situations listed below? Enter the number of the best option in the table below.

		Option number
(a)	Paying variable amounts to twenty suppliers at the end of each month	
(b)	Paying a monthly business rates bill of twelve fixed instalments of £258.90	
(c)	Buying a new car costing £34,000 for delivery the following day	
(d)	Paying an electricity bill which has variable quarterly payments	
(e)	Buying a jar of coffee for office use from the local foodstore	
(f)	A same-day payment of £350,000 to a firm of solicitors for the purchase of a new shop	

List of payment options – enter the option number in the appropriate box in the table above.

1   standing order

2   cash which you can claim back from the person who operates the petty cash system

3   bank draft

4   direct debit

5   CHAPS payment

6   BACS direct credit

1.7 Select the most appropriate payment method for each of the following descriptions:

Description	Payment method
A payment made by card where the amount is reserved immediately in the bank account	
An instruction in writing signed by the bank's customer telling the bank to pay an amount to a named person	
An electronic payment for a high value same-day payment	
An instruction to the bank to make the same regular payments from the bank account	

Choose from the following payment methods – do not use each more than once:

- BACS
- Cash
- CHAPS
- Cheque
- Credit card
- Debit card
- Direct debit
- Standing order

2 Payment methods and the bank account balance

this chapter covers...

This chapter explains how the difference in timing of various payment methods can affect the balance of the bank account of a business. The topics covered include:

- *terminology used for business bank accounts*
- *the way in which a bank overdraft works*
- *the importance of looking after a business bank account balance*
- *the costs of running a bank account*
- *the financial implications of **good** management of the bank account*
- *the financial implications of **poor** management of the bank account*
- *the need for businesses **receiving** payments to make sure that they are paid into the account sooner rather than later*
- *the policy for businesses **making** payments so that they are deducted from the account later rather than sooner*

The payment methods considered in this chapter include:

- *cash*
- *bank drafts*
- *electronic bank transfers (BACS, standing orders, direct debits, Faster Payments, CHAPS)*
- *debit cards*
- *cheques*
- *credit cards*

BUSINESS BANK ACCOUNTS – SOME TERMINOLOGY

current account – definition

A business current account can be defined as:

an account with a bank into which money can be paid and from which payments can be made

debits and credits

The important rule to remember about a bank account is that the terms 'debit' and 'credit' are the reverse way round from 'debit' and 'credit' in double-entry bookkeeping. This is because transactions in bank account are looked at from the bank's point of view.

The rule for a bank account is:

- payments **into** a bank account are known as **credits**

- payments **out of** a bank account are called **debits**

This is the opposite to double-entry bookkeeping in the cash book of a business where a receipt is a debit (left-hand side of the cash book) and a payment is a credit (right-hand side of the cash book).

debit and credit balances

A bank account has either a credit balance or a debit balance:

- a **credit balance** means that there is money in the bank account; there is a **positive** balance (the bank owes the customer)

- a **debit balance** means that there is no money in the bank account; there is a **negative** balance (the customer owes the bank)

OVERDRAFTS

There is nothing wrong about a business having a debit balance – it can in fact be very useful for a customer who needs financial assistance to have a debit (negative) balance on its current account by borrowing from the bank by means of an **overdraft**.

For example, a retail business might want to buy goods which it knows will sell quickly and make a good profit. It may not have the money available at the time but knows that it can repay any borrowing within the next few months. The simplest way of raising the money in the short term is for the business to apply to its bank for an **overdraft** of a stated amount on its current account.

the features of an overdraft

■ an arrangement which will allow the business to go 'overdrawn' (ie have a debit balance) on its bank current account

■ the authorisation from the bank will be for a certain period of time, eg 12 months, and can often be renewed at the end of that period

■ the overdraft will set an upper limit for the debit balance which can be outstanding at any one time, eg £25,000

■ with an authorised overdraft the bank account is likely to have a fluctuating balance and may 'swing' from a credit balance to a debit balance and then back into credit again

■ interest is calculated on a daily basis on the amount borrowed from the bank and the interest charge is debited to the account at regular intervals

■ a fee is normally payable when the overdraft is first arranged and also when it is renewed

An overdraft is a very flexible arrangement because the business customer can borrow whenever money is needed and can repay borrowing when money comes back into the business.

EFFICIENT BANK ACCOUNT MANAGEMENT

the costs of running a business bank account

Banks do not provide business bank accounts free of charge. Whether the balance is in credit or in debit there will be bank charges to pay.

It is a good principle for a business with a bank overdraft limit to 'manage' its bank account so that the cost to the business is kept to a minimum. The normal costs involved include:

■ bank service charges for operating the account

■ interest payable on overdrawn (debit) balances

■ fees for setting up and renewing an overdraft

the results of poor account management

Sometimes a business bank account might go overdrawn **without the authorisation of the bank**. A common example of this is when a business is having financial problems. If this happens, the bank will ask for repayment or even return as unpaid cheques that the customer has issued. There will be substantial extra charges for the business.

good practice in bank account management

Bearing these account charges in mind, it is good practice for a business to minimise costs as follows:

- keep the bank account in credit whenever possible

- if there is an authorised overdraft limit, keep the account within that limit

- **when receiving payments**: make sure that money received is paid into the account **sooner rather than later**

- **when making payments**: choose a payment method which results in the money being deducted from the account **later rather than earlier**

a note on paying 'later' rather than 'late'

Note that paying **later** rather than earlier does not mean delaying payment longer than is normally acceptable. Paying **late** could give the business a bad reputation and even result in a supplier withdrawing credit. For example, paying an invoice 30 days after the invoice date is fully acceptable if 30 days credit is allowed. Importantly, it will also provide the business with that amount of money for 30 days. But paying an invoice 60 days after the invoice date if 30 days credit is allowed is not acceptable practice.

TIMING OF PAYMENTS AND THE BANK BALANCE

A business should make best use of the various payment methods to improve solvency – the ability of a business to pay its way. It should be familiar with the time it takes for each to be processed by the appropriate payment system.

The rest of this chapter deals with the timings associated with the payment methods listed below. They are listed in order of how quickly the money for the payment will be deducted from the bank account.

- cash, bank drafts, CHAPS electronic bank transfer, Faster Payments

- BACS electronic bank transfers

- debit cards

- cheques

- credit cards

same-day deductions from the bank account

In order to keep the bank balance as high as possible for as long as possible, a business should make a same-day deduction for a payment on the latest possible date – within reason. Same-day deductions include:

■ **cash**

Any withdrawal of cash from the bank will be deducted from the account on the same day that the withdrawal is made. Examples of this include:

– top-ups of **petty cash**, ie cash kept in the office and used for small expenses incurred by the business

– payment of **wages** to employees who are paid in cash; this is also best done as late as possible because of the security risks of a business holding cash

■ **bank draft**

A bank draft – a bank 'cheque' which is seen to be as good as cash – will be deducted from the account on the day that it is issued. A bank draft is normally used for large purchases.

■ **CHAPS electronic bank transfer**

The amount of a CHAPS electronic bank transfer (a same-day bank-to-bank electronic transfer) will be deducted from the account on the day that the transfer is made. The amount is normally very large, eg paying for a property purchase.

■ **Faster Payment**

The time taken for this electronic money transfer made from one bank account to another is up to two hours, but can be as short as a few minutes. Payment can be:

– a single payment made for the same day

– a single payment authorised in advance for sending at a later date

– a standing order (regular payments on fixed dates, spread over a period of time)

■ **BACS direct credits and direct debits**

The BACS electronic bank transfer system operates on the basis that instructions are set up in advance for payment from one account to another account three working days before the payments are made. Payment is taken from the payer's bank account on the same day that it is paid into the account of the person or business receiving it. In other words, it is a same-day deduction which requires three working days' notice.

one day later deductions

■ **debit card**

Payment for a purchase made by debit card is normally debited from the bank account on the next working day following the transaction, but can take longer. Note that immediately a payment is made, the bank will reserve the funds from the available balance of the bank account.

cheques and credit cards

There are many variations in the time it takes for a cheque to be deducted from the account of the payer. It depends on when and where the person receiving the cheque pays it into the bank (note that cheques can be paid in electronically using the bank's app). The following rules apply:

■ **cheques paid in at the bank branch of the cheque issuer**

If Business A gives a cheque to Business B on Monday and Business B pays it in at Business A's bank branch on Monday, the money will be deducted from the account of Business A on the **same day**.

The rule here is:

'cheque paid in at the cheque issuer's branch – same-day payment'.

■ **cheques paid in at a different bank or bank branch**

If Business A gives a cheque to Business B on Monday and Business B pays it in at Business B's bank branch on Monday, the money will be deducted from the account of Business A **on the next working day**.

The rule here is:

'cheque paid in at different branch – payment deducted one working day later'.

The great majority of cheques are paid in at a different branch from the issuer's branch, giving businesses writing out cheques one working day's delay before the money is deducted from their bank account.

■ **cheques sent in the post**

If Business A posts a cheque to Business B on Monday using second class post, the cheque may not get to Business B until later in the week. In using this payment method, Business A will have the amount of the cheque in its bank account for up to a week before the money is deducted from its bank account.

■ **cheques with technical errors**

It may be that Business A issues a cheque to Business B with a technical error on it, for example:

– Business A has forgotten to sign it

– the amount in words and in figures is not the same

In this case the cheque may be paid into the bank by Business B but then returned by the banking system to Business A asking for it to be corrected. Business B will need to contact Business A to have the cheque corrected. It can then be paid in again. This process will take at least a week, with the result that Business A has had the extra funds in its bank account for that period.

■ **credit cards**

A company credit card is a popular way of enabling business employees such as sales representatives and employees working away to pay for business expenses as they are incurred, eg travel and accommodation costs.

The business can pay for one month's expenses in one amount by direct debit or debit card during the following month, so providing the business bank account with extra funds for the month up to the payment date. Alternatively, part can be paid with the remaining balance carried forward to next month.

the effect of different payment methods on the bank account		
payment method	**payment process**	**effect on bank account**
cash	notes and coins withdrawn from the bank	immediate reduction in balance
bank draft	'as good as cash' cheque issued by the bank	immediate reduction in balance
CHAPS payment	large amount electronic transfer by the bank	immediate reduction in balance
Faster Payment	electronic transfer processed by banks (used for immediate payments and standing orders)	immediate reduction in balance
BACS payment	electronic transfer processed by BACS set up on BACS system 3 days before the actual money transfer (used for direct credits and direct debits)	reduction in balance on the same day that the transfer reaches the account receiving payment
debit card	card used for business expenses	normally taken from the account on the next working day (but funds reserved immediately)
cheque	payment relies on an issued cheque – being sent by the issuer to the recipient – being paid into a bank by the recipient – being cleared for payment by the issuer's bank – being technically correct – not 'bounced' (returned) by the issuer's bank	amount deducted from the bank account of the cheque issuer: it can be the same day (if the cheque is paid in at the issuer's bank branch), or up to a week if it is posted to the payee
credit card	card used for business expenses	monthly payment of the previous month's expenses made on the card

Chapter Summary

- A business bank account will either have a positive balance (a 'credit balance') or a negative balance (a 'debit balance').

- An overdraft is when a bank current account is authorised by the bank to have a negative (debit) balance which will provide short-term financing to a business.

- A bank which authorises a business overdraft will set a 'limit' up to which the business can borrow.

- A business pays charges when an overdraft is set up or renewed, and interest when the account goes overdrawn.

- A business should manage its bank account balance carefully to minimise costs such as interest and charges.

- Costs can be minimised by ensuring that money due to the business is paid into the bank account promptly.

- Payments should be managed carefully in consideration of the amount of time taken between making the payment and the day on which the money is deducted from the account.

- Payments which are deducted from the account on the same day (eg cash, CHAPS, bank drafts) immediately reduce the amount of money available in the account.

- Payment methods which involve a delay in the time it takes for the deduction from the bank account (eg cheques and credit cards) provide money for a short while in the account for use by the business.

Key Terms		
	current account	a bank account into which money can be paid and from which payments can be made
	debit balance	a negative balance on a bank account; the customer is borrowing and owes the bank
	credit balance	a positive balance on a bank account; the bank owes the customer
	overdraft	an arrangement with a bank to allow short-term borrowing (debit balance) on a current account
	overdraft limit	the amount which a bank will allow a customer to borrow on an overdraft
	same-day deduction	where a payment made by a business is deducted from bank account on the same day

> **Tutorial note:** The key terms defining the various payment methods used are to be found in the previous chapter (page 12). The time intervals involved before the deductions are made from the bank account are set out in the right-hand column of the table on page 22 of this chapter.

Activities

2.1 Insert the words 'debit' or 'credit' in the correct boxes to complete the following two sentences:

(a) A positive balance on a bank account is called a [ ] balance.

(b) A negative balance on a bank account is called a [ ] balance.

2.2 Good practice in bank account management follows certain principles. Which **one** of these options is correct?

(a)	A bank account should be kept in credit whenever possible	
(b)	A bank account should be kept in debit whenever possible	

2.3 The following principle applies when paying cheques into a bank account. Which **one** of these options is correct?

(a)	Cheques should be paid in as soon as possible	
(b)	Cheques should be paid in once a month	

2.4 The following principle applies when making payments from a bank account. Which **one** of these options is correct?

(a)	Payments should be made as soon as possible	
(b)	Payments should be made later rather than earlier, but not too late	

2.5 Different types of bank payment can take different periods of time before they are deducted from the bank account.

Choose the time periods (same day/next day/next month) for the different types of payment listed below. Tick the appropriate column in the table.

		Same day	Next day	Next month
(a)	Debit card			
(b)	Cash			
(c)	CHAPS			
(d)	Credit card			
(e)	Faster Payment			

2.6 A business, Stokes Ltd, banks at Lloyds Bank, Dorchester. At a meeting on Monday a director of Stokes Ltd hands a cheque to the director of another business, Broad Ltd, to settle their account. Broad Ltd pays the cheque into its account with Barclays Bank, Dorchester, on the same day. Tick the day of that week on which the cheque will be deducted from the account of Stokes Ltd.

(a)	Tuesday	
(b)	Wednesday	
(c)	Thursday	

3 Bank reconciliation statements

this chapter covers...

The preparation of bank reconciliation statements requires a knowledge of:

■ *bank statements*

■ *cash book – covered in the Unit for Introduction to Bookkeeping*

The previous chapters have explained the various forms of bank receipts and payments.

The business cash book was covered in Chapter 9 of Introduction to Bookkeeping Tutorial. For bank reconciliation statements, it is the ability to update a cash book from the bank statement, and to total and balance the cash book, that is required.

The purpose of a bank reconciliation statement is to form the link between the balance at bank shown in the cash book of a business bookkeeping system and the balance shown on the bank statement from the bank.

The reasons why the cash book and bank statement may differ – and need reconciling – are because:

■ *there are timing differences caused by:*

— *unpresented cheques, the time delay between the business writing out a cheque and recording it in the cash book, and the cheque being entered by the bank on the bank statement*

— *outstanding lodgements, amounts paid into the bank by the business, but not yet recorded on the bank statement*

■ *the cash book has not been updated with items which appear on the bank statement and which should also appear in the cash book such as direct debits, standing orders and bank charges*

Assuming that there are no errors and both cash book and bank statement are correct, the two documents need to be reconciled with each other, ie their closing balances need to be agreed by means of a calculation known as a bank reconciliation statement.

RECEIVING THE BANK STATEMENT

When the bank statement is received – either electronically or through the post – it must be matched or compared with the cash book in order to identify any differences or discrepancies.

These differences are:

■ timing differences

■ updating items for the cash book

timing differences

The two main timing differences or discrepancies between the bank columns of the cash book and the bank statement are:

■ **unpresented cheques** – cheques issued, not yet recorded on the bank statement

■ **outstanding lodgements** – amounts paid into the bank, not yet recorded on the bank statement

The first of these – **unpresented cheques** – is caused because, when a cheque is written out, it is immediately entered on the payments side of the cash book, even though it may be a few days before the cheque is paid in by the recipient, processed by the bank and recorded on the bank statement. Therefore, for a few days at least, the cash book shows a lower balance than the bank statement in respect of this cheque. When the cheque is recorded on the bank statement, the difference will disappear. We have looked at only one cheque here, but a business may be issuing several cheques each day, and the difference between the cash book balance and the bank statement balance could be considerable.

With the second timing difference – **outstanding lodgements** – the business's cashier will record a receipt in the cash book as he or she prepares the bank paying-in slip. However, the receipt may not be recorded by the bank on the bank statement for a day or so, particularly if it is paid in late in the day, or if it is paid in at a bank other than the one at which the account is maintained.

Until the lodgement is recorded by the bank, the cash book will show a higher bank account balance than the bank statement. Once it is entered on the bank statement, the difference will disappear.

These two timing differences are involved in the calculation known as the **bank reconciliation statement**. The business cash book must not be altered because they will correct themselves on the bank statement within a few days.

updating items for the cash book

Besides the timing differences described on the previous page, there may be other differences between the bank columns of the cash book and the bank statement, and these do need to be recorded in the cash book to bring it up to date.

For example, the bank might make a standing order payment on behalf of a business – such an item is correctly deducted by the bank, and it might be that the bank statement acts as a reminder to the business cashier of the payment: it should then be entered in the cash book.

Examples of items that show in the bank statement and need to be recorded in the cash book include:

receipts – money in

- electronic receipts, including BACS direct credits, Faster Payments, and CHAPS payments
- bank interest received

payments – money out

- electronic payments made by the bank, eg standing order and direct debit payments (many businesses keep schedules of their recurring standing orders and direct debits – from these the cash book is updated as the payments fall due)
- bank charges and interest paid
- unpaid cheques deducted by the bank – for example, cheques from customers paid in by the business which are not paid by the issuer's bank

For each of these items, the cashier needs to check to see if they have been entered in the cash book; if not, they need to be recorded (provided that the bank has not made an error). If the bank has made an error, it must be notified as soon as possible and the incorrect transactions reversed by the bank in its own accounting records.

THE BANK RECONCILIATION STATEMENT

The **bank reconciliation statement** forms the link between the balances shown in the bank statement and in the cash book:

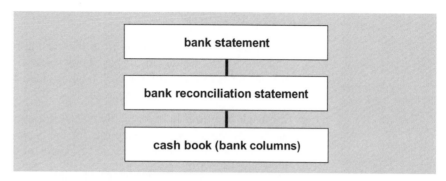

Upon receipt of a bank statement, reconciliation of the two balances is carried out in the following way:

- tick off the items that appear in both cash book and bank statement
- the unticked items on the bank statement are entered into the bank columns of the cash book to bring it up to date (provided none are errors made by the bank)
- the bank columns of the cash book are now balanced to find the revised figure
- the remaining unticked items from the cash book will be the timing differences
- the timing differences are used to prepare the bank reconciliation statement, which takes the following format (with example figures):

		£	£
XYZ TRADING LIMITED			
Bank Reconciliation Statement as at 31 October 20-1			
Closing bank statement balance			245
Less: unpresented cheques			
J Lewis	cheque no 0012378	60	
ABC Limited	cheque no 0012392	100	
Eastern Oil Company	cheque no 0012407	80	
		240	
			5
Add: outstanding lodgements			
T Mehta		220	
Padmore & Co		300	
		520	
Closing cash book balance			525

Notes:

- the layout shown above starts from the closing bank statement balance, and works towards the closing cash book balance. A common variation of this layout is to start with the cash book balance and to work towards the bank statement balance (see page 34)

- if a bank overdraft is involved, brackets or a minus sign should be used around the numbers to indicate this for the bank statement or cash book balance. The timing differences are still added or deducted, as appropriate

- once the bank reconciliation statement agrees, it should be filed because it proves that the bank statement and cash book were reconciled at a particular date. If, next time it is prepared, it fails to agree, the previous statement is proof that reconciliation was reached at that time

Case Study

BANK RECONCILIATION STATEMENT

situation

The cashier of Severn Trading Company has prepared the business's cash book for the month of February 20-1 from the digital bookkeeping system, as shown below.

Note that the cheque number is shown against payments.

Dr					Cash Book			Cr
Date	Details	Cash	Bank	Date	Details		Cash	Bank
20-1		£	£	20-1			£	£
1 Feb	Balances b/d	250.75	1,340.50	3 Feb	Appleton Ltd	123456		675.25
6 Feb	A Abbott		208.50	5 Feb	Wages		58.60	
10 Feb	Sales	145.25		12 Feb	Rent	123457		125.00
16 Feb	Sales		278.30	17 Feb	D Smith & Co	123458		421.80
20 Feb	Sales	204.35		24 Feb	Stationery		75.50	
23 Feb	D Richards Ltd		162.30	25 Feb	G Christie	123459		797.55
26 Feb	Sales		353.95		Balances c/d		466.25	586.25
27 Feb	P Paul Ltd		262.30					
		600.35	2,605.85				600.35	2,605.85
	Balances b/d	466.25	586.25					

The cash balance of £466.25 shown by the cash columns at the month-end has been agreed with the cash held in the cash box. The bank statement for February 20-1 has just been received:

| National Bank plc | | Account title | | Severn Trading |
| Bartown Branch | | | | Company |

Account number 67812318
Statement 45

Date	Details	Payments	Receipts	Balance
20-1		£	£	£
1 Feb	Balance brought forward			1340.50 Cr
7 Feb	Credit		208.50	1549.00 Cr
10 Feb	Cheque 123456	675.25		873.75 Cr
17 Feb	Credit		278.30	1152.05 Cr
17 Feb	Cheque 123457	125.00		1027.05 Cr
24 Feb	Credit		162.30	1189.35 Cr
24 Feb	BACS J Jarvis Ltd		100.00	1289.35 Cr
26 Feb	Cheque 123458	421.80		867.55 Cr
26 Feb	Direct debit A-Z Finance	150.00		717.55 Cr
27 Feb	Credit		353.95	1071.50 Cr
27 Feb	Bank charges	10.00		1061.50 Cr

solution

> It is important to note that the bank statement is prepared from the bank's viewpoint: thus a credit balance shows that the customer is a payable of the bank, ie the bank owes the balance to the customer. In the customer's own cash book, the bank is shown as a debit balance, ie an asset.

As the month-end balance at bank shown by the cash book, £586.25, is not the same as that shown by the bank statement, £1,061.50, it is necessary to compare individual items in the cash book and on the bank statement for accuracy. The steps are:

1 Tick off the items that appear in both the cash book and the bank statement.

2 The unticked items on the bank statement are recorded in the bank columns of the cash book to bring it up to date. These are:

- receipt 24 Feb BACS credit, J Jarvis Limited £100.00
- payments 26 Feb Direct debit, A-Z Finance £150.00
- 27 Feb Bank Charges, £10.00

In double-entry bookkeeping, the other part of the transaction will need to be recorded in the accounts.

3 The cash book is now balanced to find the revised closing balance:

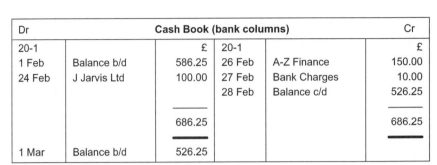

Dr			Cash Book (bank columns)			Cr
20-1		£	20-1			£
1 Feb	Balance b/d	586.25	26 Feb	A-Z Finance		150.00
24 Feb	J Jarvis Ltd	100.00	27 Feb	Bank Charges		10.00
			28 Feb	Balance c/d		526.25
		_____				_____
		686.25				686.25
		▬▬▬				▬▬▬
1 Mar	Balance b/d	526.25				

4 The remaining unticked items from the cash book are:

- receipt   27 Feb – P Paul Limited £262.30

- payment   25 Feb – G Christie (cheque no 123459) £797.55

These items are timing differences, which should appear on next month's bank statement. They will be used in the bank reconciliation statement.

5 The bank reconciliation statement is now prepared, starting with the bank statement balance of £1,061.50 and using the unticked items from the cash book which were noted above.

SEVERN TRADING COMPANY

Bank Reconciliation Statement as at 28 February 20-1

	£
Closing bank statement balance	1,061.50
Less: unpresented cheque, no 123459	797.55
	_____
	263.95
Add: outstanding lodgement, P Paul Limited	262.30
	_____
Closing cash book balance	526.25

This bank reconciliation statement starts with the closing bank statement balance, and finishes with the amended closing balance from the cash book, ie the two figures are reconciled.

notes on the case study

- the unpresented cheque is deducted from the closing bank statement balance because, until it is recorded by the bank, the bank statement shows a higher balance than the cash book

- the outstanding lodgement is added to the bank statement balance because, until it is recorded by the bank, the bank statement shows a lower balance than the cash book

PREPARING A BANK RECONCILIATION STATEMENT

In order to help with the Activities at the end of the chapter, here is a step-by-step summary of the procedure. Reconciliation of the bank statement balance with that shown in the cash book should be carried out in the following way:

1 From the bank columns of the cash book tick off, in both cash book and bank statement, the receipts that appear in both.

2 From the bank columns of the cash book tick off, in both cash book and bank statement, the payments that appear in both.

3 Identify the items that are unticked on the bank statement and record them in the cash book on the debit or credit side, as appropriate. (If, however, the bank has made a mistake and debited or credited an amount in error, this should not be recorded in the cash book, but should be notified to the bank for them to make the correction. The amount will need to be shown on the bank reconciliation statement.)

4 The bank columns of the cash book are now balanced to find the up-to-date balance.

5 Start the bank reconciliation statement with the closing balance figure shown on the bank statement.

6 In the bank reconciliation statement, deduct the unticked payments shown in the cash book – these will be unpresented cheques.

7 In the bank reconciliation statement, add the unticked receipts shown in the cash book – these are outstanding lodgements.

8 The resulting money amount shown on the bank reconciliation statement is the closing cash book balance.

The layout which is often used for the bank reconciliation statement is that shown in the Case Study on the previous page. The layout starts with the closing bank statement balance and finishes with the closing cash book balance. However, there is no reason why it should not commence with the closing cash book balance and finish with the closing bank statement balance: with this layout it is necessary to:

■ *add* unpresented cheques

■ *deduct* outstanding lodgements

The bank reconciliation statement of Severn Trading Company would then appear as (see the next page):

```
┌─────────────────────────────────────────────────────────────────┐
│                   SEVERN TRADING COMPANY                          │
│         Bank Reconciliation Statement as at 28 February 20-1      │
│                                                            £      │
│  Closing cash book balance                              526.25    │
│  Add: unpresented cheque, no 123459                     797.55    │
│                                                        _____   │
│                                                        1,323.80   │
│  Less: outstanding lodgement, P Paul Limited            262.30    │
│                                                        _____   │
│  Closing bank statement balance                        1,061.50   │
│                                                        ━━━━━━━━    │
└─────────────────────────────────────────────────────────────────┘
```

DEALING WITH UNUSUAL ITEMS ON BANK STATEMENTS

The following are some of the unusual features that may occur on bank statements. As with other accounting discrepancies, where they cannot be resolved they should be referred to the accounts supervisor for guidance.

out-of-date cheques

These are cheques that are more than six months old. The bank will not pay such cheques, so they can be recorded back in the cash book, ie debit cash book (and credit the other double-entry account involved).

unpaid cheques

A cheque received by a business is recorded as a receipt in the cash book and then paid into the bank, but it may not be paid by the issuer's bank because:

■ the issuer of the cheque has stopped it

■ the issuer has insufficient money in the bank (a 'dishonoured' cheque)

■ there is a technical problem with the cheque, eg it is not signed

A cheque unpaid in this way should be recorded in the bookkeeping system:

■ as a payment in the cash book on the credit side, and

    – either as a debit to receivables ledger control account (if it is a credit sale), and a debit to the trade receivable's account in receivables ledger

    – or as a debit to sales account (if it is a cash sale)

bank errors

Errors made by the bank can include:

■ **a cheque deducted from the bank account which has not been issued by the business** – look for a cheque number on the bank statement that is different from the current cheque series: take care, though, as it could be a cheque from an old cheque book

- **an electronic receipt, eg a BACS credit, shown on the bank statement for which the business is not the correct recipient**; if in doubt, the bank will be able to give further details of the sender of the money

- **standing orders and direct debits paid at the wrong time or for the wrong amounts** – a copy of all standing order and direct debit authorisations sent to the bank should be kept by the business for reference purposes; standing order and direct debit schedules should be kept up-to-date so that the cash book can be updated as recurring payments fall due

When an error is found, it should be queried immediately with the bank. The item and amount should not be recorded in the business's cash book until it has been resolved. If, in the meantime, a bank reconciliation statement is to be prepared, the bank error should be shown separately. When the reconciliation is from the bank statement balance to the cash book balance, add payments and deduct receipts that the bank has applied to the account incorrectly.

bank interest received

For certain types of accounts, banks may pay interest to their customers. When this happens the bank statement of the customer shows a receipt for 'interest received' or 'bank interest received'.

bank charges and interest paid

From time to time banks charge customers' accounts with an amount for:

- service charges, ie the cost of operating the bank account

- interest paid, ie the borrowing cost when the bank account is overdrawn

On a bank statement, such items are shown in the 'payments' or 'paid out' column.

IMPORTANT: OPENING BALANCE DIFFERENCES

If you look back to the Case Study on pages 30-32, you will see that both the cash book (bank columns) and the bank statement balance both started the month with the same balance: 1 February 20-1 £1,340.50.

In reality, it is unlikely that the opening cash book and bank statement balances will be the same – there will be an opening balance difference. It will be necessary, in these circumstances, to prepare a simple opening bank reconciliation statement in order to prove that there are no errors between cash book and bank statement at the start of the reconciliation period.

This is set out in the same format as the end-of-month bank reconciliation statement, and is best prepared immediately after ticking off the items that appear in both cash book and bank statement. The earliest unpresented cheques and outstanding lodgements will, most probably, be causing the difference. Of course, where last month's bank reconciliation statement is available, there is no need to prepare an opening reconciliation.

There is usually no need to prepare a formal opening bank reconciliation statement as any discrepancy in opening balances can be resolved quickly by checking the bank statement for the earliest receipts and payments. See Activities 3.5, 3.7 and 3.8.

REASONS FOR BANK RECONCILIATION STATEMENTS

■ In the preparation of a bank reconciliation statement, the transactions in the bank columns of the cash book are compared with those recorded on the bank statement. In this way, any errors in the cash book or bank statement will be found and can be corrected (or advised to the bank, if the bank statement is wrong).

■ The bank statement is an independent accounting record; therefore it will assist in deterring fraud by providing a means of verifying the cash book balance.

■ By bringing the cash book up-to-date, the business has an amended figure for the bank balance to be shown in the trial balance and financial statements.

■ It is good business practice to prepare a bank reconciliation statement each time a bank statement is received. The reconciliation statement should be prepared as quickly as possible so that any queries – either with the bank statement or in the cash book – can be resolved. Many businesses will specify to their accounting staff the timescales for preparing bank reconciliation statements – as a guideline, if the bank statement is received weekly, then the reconciliation statement should be prepared within five working days.

Chapter Summary

■ The purpose of a bank reconciliation statement is to reconcile the balance shown by the bank statement with that shown by the bank columns of the cash book.

■ Certain differences between the two are timing differences. The main timing differences are:
 – unpresented cheques
 – outstanding lodgements

These differences will be corrected by time and, most probably, will be recorded on the next bank statement.

■ Certain differences appearing on the bank statement need to be recorded in the cash book to bring it up-to-date. These include:

Receipts   –   electronic receipts, including BACS direct credits received by the bank

        –   bank interest received

Payments   –   electronic payments made by the bank, including standing order and direct debit payments

        –   bank charges and interest paid

        –   unpaid cheques deducted by the bank

■ The bank reconciliation statement makes use of the timing differences.

■ Opening balance differences are where the opening cash book balance differs from that of the opening bank statement balance.

■ Once prepared, a bank reconciliation statement is proof that the bank statement and the cash book (bank columns) were agreed at a particular date.

Key Terms		
bank reconciliation statement	forms the link between the balances shown in the bank statement and the cash book
timing differences	discrepancies between the bank statement and the cash book that will be corrected over time, such as unpresented cheques and outstanding lodgements
unpresented cheques	cheques drawn, but not yet recorded on the bank statement
outstanding lodgements	amounts paid into the bank, but not yet recorded on the bank statement
direct debit/standing order schedules	lists of direct debit and standing order payments, kept by a business, from which the cash book is updated as recurring payments fall due

Activities

3.1   When preparing a bank reconciliation statement, which **one** of the following is a timing difference?

(a)	Unpresented cheques	
(b)	Direct debit payments	
(c)	Bank charges and interest	
(d)	BACS direct credits	

3.2   A business's bank statement shows a balance of £400 in the bank. Unpresented cheques total £700; outstanding lodgements total £200. What is the balance at the bank shown by the cash book?

Tick the correct option.

(a)	£100 credit	
(b)	£200 debit	
(c)	£250 debit	
(d)	£400 debit	

3.3   The bank columns of Tom Reid's cash book for December 20-2 are as follows:

20-2	Receipts	£	20-2	Payments		£
1 Dec	Balance b/d	280	9 Dec	W Smith	345123	40
13 Dec	P Jones	30	13 Dec	Rent	345124	50
17 Dec	H Homer	72	16 Dec	Wages	345125	85
29 Dec	J Hill	13	20 Dec	B Kay	345126	320
31 Dec	Balance c/d	100				
		495				495

He then received his bank statement which showed the following transactions for December 20-2:

BANK STATEMENT		Payments	Receipts	Balance
20-2		£	£	£
1 Dec	Balance brought forward			280 CR
13 Dec	Credit		30	310 CR
15 Dec	Cheque no 345123	40		270 CR
17 Dec	Cheque no 345124	50		220 CR
22 Dec	BACS credit: H Homer		72	292 CR
23 Dec	Cheque no 345125	85		207 CR

You are to prepare a bank reconciliation statement which agrees the closing bank statement balance with the closing cash book balance.

3.4 The bank columns of P Gerrard's cash book for January 20-3 are as follows:

20-3	Receipts	£	20-3	Payments		£
1 Jan	Balance b/d	800.50	2 Jan	A Arthur Ltd	001351	100.00
6 Jan	J Baker	495.60	9 Jan	C Curtis	001352	398.50
30 Jan	G Shotton Ltd	335.75	13 Jan	Donald & Co	001353	229.70
			14 Jan	Bryant & Sons	001354	312.00
			23 Jan	P Reid	001355	176.50

He received his bank statement which showed the following transactions for January 20-3:

BANK STATEMENT		Payments	Receipts	Balance
20-3		£	£	£
1 Jan	Balance brought forward			800.50 CR
6 Jan	Cheque no 001351	100.00		700.50 CR
6 Jan	Credit		495.60	1,196.10 CR
13 Jan	BACS credit: T K Supplies		716.50	1,912.60 CR
20 Jan	Cheque no 001352	398.50		1,514.10 CR
23 Jan	Direct debit: Omni Finance	207.95		1,306.15 CR
26 Jan	Cheque no 001353	229.70		1,076.45 CR
31 Jan	Bank interest		5.50	1,081.95 CR

You are to:

(a) Check the items on the bank statement against the items in the cash book and update the cash book accordingly; total the cash book and show the balance carried down at 31 January 20-3.

(b) Prepare a bank reconciliation statement at 31 January 20-3 which agrees the closing bank statement balance with the closing cash book balance.

3.5 The bank columns of Jane Doyle's cash book for May 20-4 are as follows:

20-4	Receipts	£	20-4	Payments		£
1 May	Balance b/d	300	3 May	P Stone	867714	28
7 May	Cash	162	14 May	Alpha Ltd	867715	50
17 May	C Brewster	89	28 May	E Deakin	867716	110
27 May	Cash	60				
28 May	Cash	40				

She received her bank statement which showed the following transactions for May 20-4:

BANK STATEMENT		Payments	Receipts	Balance
20-4		£	£	£
1 May	Balance brought forward			400 CR
2 May	Cheque no 867713	100		300 CR
5 May	Cheque no 867714	28		272 CR
7 May	Credit		162	434 CR
17 May	Standing order: A-Z Insurance	25		409 CR
19 May	BACS credit		89	498 CR
20 May	Cheque no 867715	50		448 CR
27 May	Credit		60	508 CR
31 May	Bank Charges	10		498 CR

Tutorial note: there is an opening balance difference – see page 35 for guidance.

You are to:

(a) Update the cash book to 31 May 20-4, and show the balance carried down.

(b) Prepare a bank reconciliation statement at 31 May 20-4 which agrees the closing bank statement balance with the closing cash book balance.

3.6 Identify whether each of the following statements is true or false.

Statement	True	False
Unpresented cheques, outstanding lodgements and bank charges are all examples of timing differences		
A direct debit for car insurance of £325 is shown on the bank statement but is not entered in the cash book. This amount will need to be deducted in the bank reconciliation to make it agree with the cash book		
Comparing the debit side of the cash book with receipts on the bank statement will enable BACS and other automated payments missing from the cash book to be identified		

3.7   On 4 June Milestone Motors received a bank statement which showed the following transactions for May 20-5:

BANK STATEMENT		Paid out	Paid in	Balance
20-5		£	£	£
1 May	Balance brought forward			3,802 C
2 May	Cheque no 451761	150		3,652 C
10 May	Cheque no 451762	751		2,901 C
11 May	Cheque no 451763	268		2,633 C
13 May	Cheque no 451765	1,045		1,588 C
14 May	BACS credit: Perran Taxis		2,596	4,184 C
18 May	Direct debit: Wyvern Council	198		3,986 C
20 May	Direct debit: A1 Insurance	1,005		2,981 C
25 May	Direct debit: Okaro and Company	254		2,727 C
25 May	Bank charges	20		2,707 C
D = Debit C = Credit				

The cash book of Milestone Motors as at 31 May 20-5 is shown below:

CASH BOOK

Date	Details	Bank	Date	Cheque no	Details	Bank
20-5		£	20-5			£
1 May	Balance b/f	3,652	4 May	451762	Smith and Company	751
26 May	J Ackland	832	4 May	451763	Bryant Limited	268
28 May	Stamp Limited	1,119	7 May	451764	Curtis Cars	1,895
			7 May	451765	Parts Supplies	1,045

Tutorial note: there is an opening balance difference – see page 35 for guidance.

You are to:

(a)   Check the items on the bank statement against the items in the cash book.

(b)   Update the cash book as needed.

(c)   Total the cash book and show clearly the balance carried down at 31 May and brought down at 1 June.

(d)   Prepare a bank reconciliation statement at 31 May 20-5 which agrees the closing bank statement balance with the closing cash book balance.

3.8   On 30 June Durning Trading received a bank statement as at 27 June 20-8:

BANK STATEMENT		Paid out	Paid in	Balance
20-8		£	£	£
1 Jun	Balance brought forward			768 C
2 Jun	Cheque 364125	427		341 C
3 Jun	BACS credit: Asif Ltd		1,122	1,463 C
18 Jun	Cheque 364127	4,200		2,737 D
20 Jun	Direct debit: JC Property Co	850		3,587 D
23 Jun	BACS credit: Sand & Stone		2,486	1,101 D
26 Jun	BACS credit: Surfrider Ltd		4,110	3,009 C
27 Jun	Direct debit: Vord Finance	275		2,734 C
27 Jun	Cheque 364128	1,062		1,672 C
D = Debit C = Credit				

The cash book of Durning Trading as at 27 June 20-8 is shown below:

CASH BOOK

Date	Details	Bank	Date	Cheque no	Details	Bank
20-8		£	20-8			£
1 Jun	Balance b/d	1,890	1 Jun	364125	Penryn Ltd	427
20 Jun	Chiverton Ltd	1,200	3 Jun	364126	Fal Boats	760
24 Jun	Perran Ltd	4,750	10 Jun	364127	S Mawes	4,200
24 Jun	P Porth	8,950	20 Jun	364128	Castle Supplies	1,062
			27 Jun		Balance c/d	10,341

You are to update the cash book and to prepare a bank reconciliation statement at 27 June 20-8 (see next page).

Cash book	Debit	Credit
	£	£
Closing balance b/d	10,341	
Adjustments:		
Adjusted balance c/d		

Bank reconciliation	£
Closing bank statement balance	1,672
Less unpresented cheques:	
Add outstanding lodgements:	
Adjusted closing cash book balance	

4 Use of control accounts

this chapter covers...

In this chapter we look at control accounts which are used as 'master' accounts to control a number of subsidiary accounts.

A control account (also known as a totals account) records the total of transactions passing through the subsidiary (memorandum) accounts. In this way, the balance of the control account always equals (unless an error has occurred) the total balances of the subsidiary accounts.

The three control accounts we study in this chapter are:

■ *receivables ledger control account – the total of receivables/trade receivables*

■ *payables ledger control account – the total of payables/trade payables*

■ *Value Added Tax control account – the total of VAT due to or from HM Revenue & Customs*

The chapter explains:

■ *the purpose of control accounts*

■ *how control accounts work*

■ *reconciling control accounts to subsidiary accounts*

■ *the layout of control accounts*

■ *how control accounts fit into the accounting system*

■ *information sources for control accounts*

THE PURPOSE OF CONTROL ACCOUNTS

Control accounts are 'master' accounts which control a number of subsidiary (memorandum) accounts – individual supplier or customer accounts, for example. This set-up can be illustrated as follows:

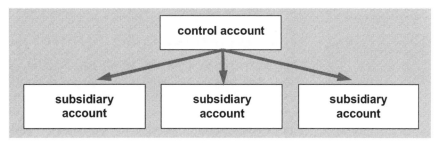

The control account (also known as a **totals account**) is used to record the totals of transactions passing through the subsidiary accounts. In this way, the balance of the control account is always equal to the total balances of the subsidiary accounts, unless an error has occurred.

Three commonly-used control accounts in an accounting system are:

■ **receivables ledger control account**, which controls the receivables ledger

■ **payables ledger control account**, which controls the payables ledger

■ **Value Added Tax control account**, which brings together totals of VAT from books of prime entry, such as the day books and cash book

Note: each of these control accounts is a general ledger account in the accounting system.

In the illustration above we have seen how a control account acts as a master account for a number of subsidiary accounts. The principle is that, if the total of the opening balances for subsidiary accounts is known, together with the total of amounts increasing these balances, and the total of amounts decreasing these balances, then the total of the closing balances for the subsidiary accounts can be calculated.

For example:

	£
Total of opening balances	50,000
Add increases	10,000
	60,000
Less decreases	12,000
Total of closing balances	48,000

The total of the closing balances can now be reconciled (agreed) with a separate listing of the balances of the subsidiary accounts to ensure that the two figures agree. If they do, it proves that the ledgers within the section are correct, unless an error has occurred within the ledger section.

RECEIVABLES LEDGER CONTROL ACCOUNT

how receivables ledger control account works

The diagram on the next page shows the subsidiary accounts which form the receivables ledger of a particular business – in practice there would be more than four trade receivables' (customers') accounts involved. The receivables ledger control account acts as a totals account, which records totals of the transactions passing through the accounts which it controls. Note that transactions are shown in the control account **on the same side** as in the subsidiary accounts.

Receivables ledger control account is reconciled with the balances of the subsidiary accounts which it controls. Thus, control accounts act as an aid to locating errors: if the control account and subsidiary accounts agree, then the error is likely to lie elsewhere. In this way the control account acts as an intermediate checking device – proving the arithmetical accuracy of the ledger section unless an error has occurred within the ledger section.

reasons for reconciling receivables ledger control account

At regular intervals – eg weekly or monthly – it is important that a business reconciles the balances of subsidiary accounts in receivables ledger with the balance of receivables ledger control account. To carry out this reconciliation, the balances of the subsidiary accounts in receivables ledger are listed and then totalled – the total should agree with the balance of receivables ledger control account. Any discrepancy (see page 53) should be investigated immediately and the error(s) traced.

Using the accounts shown on the next page, the receivables ledger control account and the subsidiary receivables ledger accounts will be reconciled at the beginning and end of the month, as follows:

Reconciliation of receivables ledger control account		
	1 January 20-4	31 January 20-4
	£	£
A Ackroyd	100	150
B Barnes	200	200
C Cox	50	180
D Douglas	150	150
Receivables ledger control account	500	680

GENERAL LEDGER

Dr			Receivables ledger control account			Cr
20-4			£	20-4		£
1 Jan	Balance b/d		500	31 Jan	Bank	443
31 Jan	Sales		700	31 Jan	Discounts allowed	7
				31 Jan	Sales returns	70
				31 Jan	Balance c/d	680
			———			———
			1,200			1,200
1 Feb	Balance b/d		680			

RECEIVABLES LEDGER

Dr		A Ackroyd			Cr
20-4		£	20-4		£
1 Jan	Balance b/d	100	12 Jan	Bank	98
6 Jan	Sales	150	12 Jan	Discounts allowed	2
			31 Jan	Balance c/d	150
		———			———
		250			250
1 Feb	Balance b/d	150			

Dr		B Barnes			Cr
20-4		£	20-4		£
1 Jan	Balance b/d	200	13 Jan	Bank	195
6 Jan	Sales	250	13 Jan	Discounts allowed	5
			27 Jan	Sales returns	50
			31 Jan	Balance c/d	200
		———			———
		450			450
1 Feb	Balance b/d	200			

Dr		C Cox			Cr
20-4		£	20-4		£
1 Jan	Balance b/d	50	20 Jan	Bank	50
15 Jan	Sales	200	29 Jan	Sales returns	20
			31 Jan	Balance c/d	180
		———			———
		250			250
1 Feb	Balance b/d	180			

Dr		D Douglas			Cr
20-4		£	20-4		£
1 Jan	Balance b/d	150	30 Jan	Bank	100
20 Jan	Sales	100	31 Jan	Balance c/d	150
		———			———
		250			250
1 Feb	Balance b/d	150			

receivables ledger control account explained

The layout of the receivables ledger control account is shown below, with sample figures.

Study the layout carefully and then read the text which follows:

Dr		Receivables ledger control account		Cr
	£			£
Balance b/d	2,900	Payments received from customers		12,100
Credit sales	14,000	Discounts allowed		290
Returned cheques	930	Sales returns		870
		Irrecoverable debts written off		1,590
		Set-off/contra entries		250
		Balance c/d		2,730
	17,830			17,830
Balance b/d	2,730			

balance b/d

The figure for balance b/d on the debit side of the control account represents the total of the balances of the individual trade receivables' accounts in the receivables ledger. This principle has been seen in the diagram on page 47. Remember that, at the end of the month (or other period covered by the control account), the account must be balanced and carried down (on the credit side) on the last day of the month, and then brought down (on the debit side) on the first day of the next month.

Note that it is possible for a customer's account to have a credit balance, instead of the usual debit balance. This may come about, for example, because the customer has paid for goods and then returned them, or has overpaid in error: the business owes the amount due, ie the customer has a credit balance for the time being. Digital bookkeeping systems usually 'net off' any such credit balances against the debit balances to give an overall figure for trade receivables.

credit sales

Only credit sales – and not cash sales – are entered in the control account because only credit sales are recorded in the customers' accounts. However, the total sales of a business may well comprise both credit and cash sales.

unpaid cheques

If a customer's cheque is unpaid, then authorisation for the entries to be made in the accounting system must be given by the accounts supervisor. These entries are:

– *debit* receivables ledger control account

– *credit* cash book (bank columns)

The transaction must also be recorded in the customer's account in the receivables ledger – on the debit side.

Note that the unpaid cheque is the prime document for the adjustment – like other prime documents, it should be stored securely for future reference.

irrecoverable debts written off

An irrecoverable debt is a debt owing to a business which it considers will never be paid.

We will look in more detail at irrecoverable debts written off in the next chapter. For the moment the accounting entries after a debt has been authorised for write off are:

– *debit* irrecoverable debts account

– *debit* Value Added Tax account (if appropriate)

– *credit* receivables ledger control account

The transaction must also be recorded in the customer's account in receivables ledger – on the credit side.

set-off/contra entries

These entries occur when the same person or business has a subsidiary account in both the receivables ledger and the payables ledger, ie they are both buying from, and selling to, the business whose accounts we are preparing.

Set-off contra entries are looked at in more detail on page 60, where we will see the entries which affect the control accounts.

receivables ledger control account in the accounting system

The diagram on the next page shows how receivables ledger control account is incorporated in the general ledger of the accounting system, with the trade receivables' accounts kept as subsidiary accounts in receivables ledger.

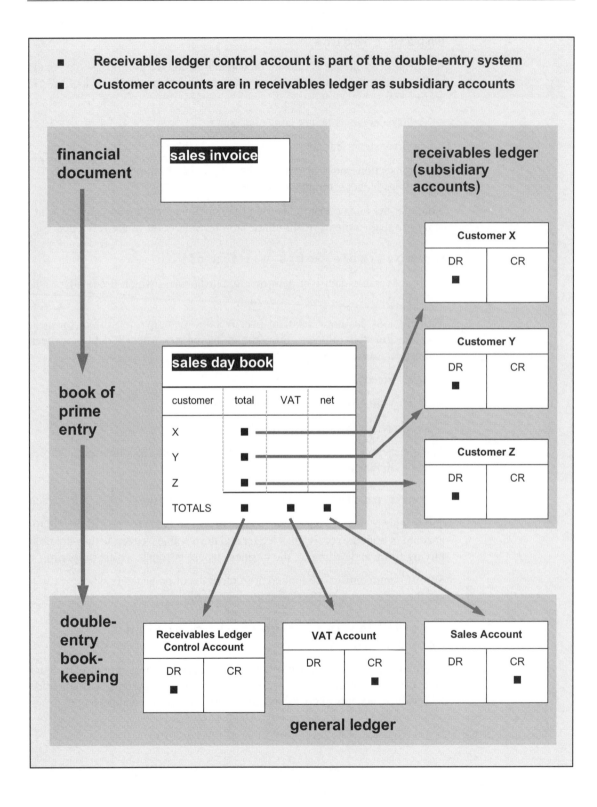

At regular intervals, the balances of the receivables ledger subsidiary accounts are reconciled with the balance of receivables ledger control account, and any discrepancies investigated.

information sources for receivables ledger control account

Control accounts use totals (remember that their other name is 'totals accounts') for the week, month, quarter or year – depending on what time period is decided upon by the business. The totals for receivables ledger control account come from a number of sources in the accounting system:

- total credit sales (including VAT) – from the total column of the sales day book

- total sales returns (including VAT) – from the total column of the sales returns day book

- total payments received from customers – from the total column of the analysed cash book

- total discounts allowed – from the total column of the discounts allowed day book

- irrecoverable debts – from the journal, or irrecoverable debts written off account (see Chapter 5)

using an aged trade receivables analysis

An **aged trade receivables analysis** is a summary of each trade receivable balance from receivables ledger analysed into columns showing how long the amounts have been outstanding. It is used by a business to show which customers are slow in paying and enables the business to decide which customers to chase for payment.

An example of an aged trade receivables analysis is given below.

Wyvern Trading Aged trade receivables analysis at 30 September 20-6				
Trade receivable	Total	0-30 days	31-60 days	61+ days
	£	£	£	£
Adams Ltd	3,510	0	0	3,510
T Brewster	1,840	1,620	220	0
Harrison & Co	760	760	0	0
D Miller	2,330	330	2,000	0
Totals	8,440	2,710	2,220	3,510

An aged trade receivables analysis is easily accessed from a digital bookkeeping system.

The analysis is normally produced at the end of each month when statements are issued to customers. From the analysis (see previous page), the business decides which customers it is going to chase up, and how. It may send a letter, an email, or it may telephone the customer. For example, from the above aged trade receivables analysis, the account of Adams Ltd is overdue for payment and a strongly worded letter or email, followed up with a telephone call, might be needed; most of the balance of D Miller's account is now overdue and a letter or email might be sent as a reminder; the account of T Brewster is partly overdue but it is unlikely that any action will be taken this month; the account of Harrison & Co is 'in order'.

dealing with discrepancies

As stated earlier, it is important at regular intervals to reconcile the balances of subsidiary accounts in receivables ledger with the balance of receivables ledger control account. The diagram on page 53 shows where error(s) might occur. The first thing to do is to establish:

■ is the balance of receivables ledger control account greater than the total of the balances of the subsidiary accounts in receivables ledger?

  or

■ is the total of the balances of the subsidiary accounts in receivables ledger greater than the balance of receivables ledger control account?

Once this has been established, the relevant column from the diagram indicates what may have caused the discrepancy. The discrepancy can then be investigated, the error(s) traced and any problems solved quickly and professionally.

PAYABLES LEDGER CONTROL ACCOUNT

how payables ledger control account works

The diagram on page 54 shows the subsidiary (memorandum) accounts which form the payables ledger of a particular business – in practice there would be more than four trade payables' (suppliers') accounts involved.

Payables ledger control account acts as a totals account: it records totals of the transactions passing through the subsidiary accounts which it controls. Note that transactions are shown in the control account on the same side as in the subsidiary accounts.

continued on page 55

Discrepancies between receivables ledger control account (rlca) and receivables ledger (rl)		
possible discrepancy	rlca greater than rl	rl greater than rlca
credit sales		
– omitted/understated in rlca	✗	✔
– omitted/understated in rl	✔	✗
– entered twice/overstated in rlca	✔	✗
– entered twice/overstated in rl	✗	✔
sales returns		
– omitted/understated in rlca	✔	✗
– omitted/understated in rl	✗	✔
– entered twice/overstated in rlca	✗	✔
– entered twice/overstated in rl	✔	✗
money received from trade receivables		
– omitted/understated in rlca	✔	✗
– omitted/understated in rl	✗	✔
– entered twice/overstated in rlca	✗	✔
– entered twice/overstated in rl	✔	✗
discounts allowed		
– omitted/understated in rlca	✔	✗
– omitted/understated in rl	✗	✔
– entered twice/overstated in rlca	✗	✔
– entered twice/overstated in rl	✔	✗
irrecoverable debts written off		
– omitted/understated in rlca	✔	✗
– omitted/understated in rl	✗	✔
– entered twice/overstated in rlca	✗	✔
– entered twice/overstated in rl	✔	✗
other		
– debit balance recorded in error as credit in rl	✔	✗
– credit balance recorded in error as debit in rl	✗	✔

GENERAL LEDGER

Dr			Payables ledger control account			Cr
20-4		£	20-4			£
31 Jan	Purchases returns	150	1 Jan	Balance b/d		1,000
31 Jan	Bank	594	31 Jan	Purchases		1,700
31 Jan	Discounts received	6				
31 Jan	Balance c/d	1,950				
		2,700				2,700
			1 Feb	Balance b/d		1,950

PAYABLES LEDGER

Dr			F Francis			Cr
20-4		£	20-4			£
16 Jan	Bank	98	1 Jan	Balance b/d		100
16 Jan	Discounts received	2	2 Jan	Purchases		200
31 Jan	Balance c/d	200				
		300				300
			1 Feb	Balance b/d		200

Dr			G Gold			Cr
20-4		£	20-4			£
15 Jan	Purchases returns	50	1 Jan	Balance b/d		200
28 Jan	Bank	100	9 Jan	Purchases		300
31 Jan	Balance c/d	350				
		500				500
			1 Feb	Balance b/d		350

Dr			H Harris			Cr
20-4		£	20-4			£
28 Jan	Purchases returns	100	1 Jan	Balance b/d		300
30 Jan	Bank	200	16 Jan	Purchases		500
31 Jan	Balance c/d	500				
		800				800
			1 Feb	Balance b/d		500

Dr			I Ingram			Cr
20-4		£	20-4			£
22 Jan	Bank	196	1 Jan	Balance b/d		400
22 Jan	Discounts received	4	27 Jan	Purchases		700
31 Jan	Balance c/d	900				
		1,100				1,100
			1 Feb	Balance b/d		900

reasons for reconciling payables ledger control account

At regular intervals – eg weekly or monthly – it is important that a business reconciles the balances of subsidiary accounts in payables ledger with the balance of payables ledger control account. To carry out this reconciliation, the balances of the subsidiary accounts in payables ledger are listed and then totalled – the total should agree with the balance of payables ledger control account. Any discrepancy should be investigated immediately and the error(s) traced.

From the diagram on the previous page, the payables ledger control account and the subsidiary payables ledger accounts will be reconciled at the beginning and end of the month, as follows:

Reconciliation of payables ledger control account		
	1 January 20-4	*31 January 20-4*
	£	£
F Francis	100	200
G Gold	200	350
H Harris	300	500
I Ingram	400	900
Payables ledger control account	1,000	1,950

payables ledger control account explained

The layout of the payables ledger control account is shown below, with sample figures.

Study the layout carefully and then read the text on the next page.

Dr		Payables ledger control account		Cr
	£			£
Payments made to suppliers	8,200	Balance b/d		5,000
Discounts received	260	Credit purchases		8,500
Purchases returns	1,070			
Set-off/contra entries	250			
Balance c/d	3,720			
	13,500			13,500
		Balance b/d		3,720

balance b/d

The figure for balance b/d on the credit side of the control account represents the total of the balances of the individual trade payables' accounts in the payables ledger. This principle has been seen in the diagram on page 54.

Note that it is possible for a supplier's account to have a debit balance, instead of the usual credit balance. This may come about, for example, if the supplier has been overpaid. Digital bookkeeping systems usually 'net off' any such debit balances against the credit balances to give an overall figure for suppliers.

credit purchases

Only credit purchases – and not cash purchases – are entered in the control account because only credit purchases are recorded in the suppliers' accounts. However, the total purchases of a business may well comprise both credit and cash purchases.

set-off/contra entries

These entries occur when the same person or business has a subsidiary account in both the payables ledger and the receivables ledger, ie they are both selling to, and buying from, the business whose accounts we are preparing.

Set-off/contra entries are looked at in more detail in the next section (page 60), where we will see the entries which affect the control accounts.

payables ledger control account in the accounting system

The diagram on the next page shows how payables ledger control account is incorporated in the general ledger of the accounting system, with the trade payables' accounts kept as subsidiary accounts in the payables ledger.

At regular intervals, the balances of the payables ledger subsidiary accounts are agreed with the balance of payables ledger control account, and any discrepancies investigated.

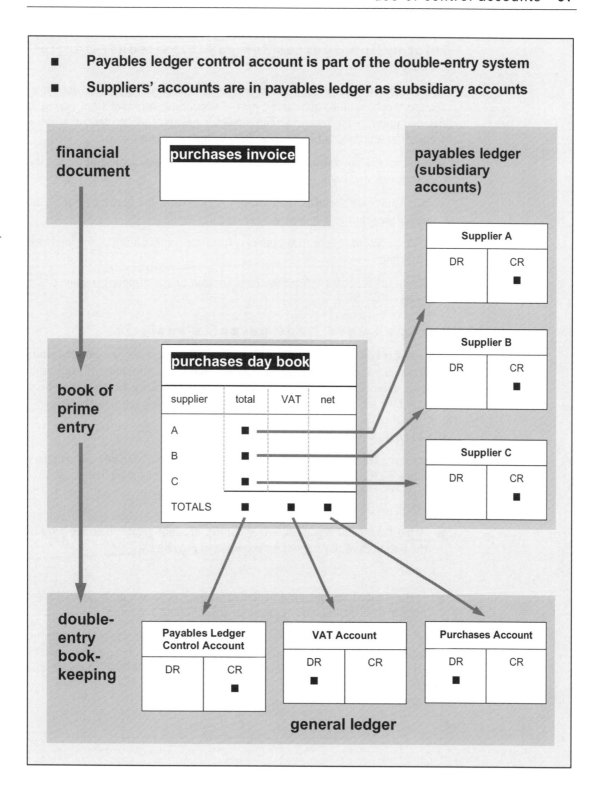

information sources for payables ledger control account

Control accounts use totals (remember that their other name is totals accounts) for the week, month, quarter or year – depending on what time period is decided upon by the business. The totals for payables ledger control account come from a number of sources in the accounting system:

- total credit purchases (including VAT) – from the total column of the purchases day book

- total purchases returns (including VAT) – from the total column of the purchases returns day book

- total payments made to suppliers – from the total column of the analysed cash book

- discounts received – from the total column of the discounts received day book

using an aged trade payables analysis

An **aged trade payables analysis** works in the same way as an aged trade receivables analysis (see page 51), except that it is a summary of each trade payable balance. It is used by a business to show how long accounts have been outstanding and it enables the business to decide which suppliers to pay.

dealing with discrepancies

As we have seen earlier, it is important to reconcile the balances of subsidiary accounts in payables ledger with the balance of payables ledger control account. The diagram on the next page shows where error(s) might occur. The first thing to do is to establish:

- is the balance of payables ledger control account greater than the total of the balances of the subsidiary accounts in payables ledger?

  or

- is the total of the balances of the subsidiary accounts in payables ledger greater than the balance of payables ledger control account?

Once this has been established, the relevant column from the diagram indicates what may have caused the discrepancy. The discrepancy can then be investigated, the error(s) traced and any problems solved quickly and professionally.

Discrepancies between payables ledger control account (plca) and payables ledger (pl)		
possible discrepancy	plca greater than pl	pl greater than plca
credit purchases		
– omitted/understated in plca	✗	✔
– omitted/understated in pl	✔	✗
– entered twice/overstated in plca	✔	✗
– entered twice/overstated in pl	✗	✔
purchases returns		
– omitted/understated in plca	✔	✗
– omitted/understated in pl	✗	✔
– entered twice/overstated in plca	✗	✔
– entered twice/overstated in pl	✔	✗
money paid to trade payables		
– omitted/understated in plca	✔	✗
– omitted/understated in pl	✗	✔
– entered twice/overstated in plca	✗	✔
– entered twice/overstated in pl	✔	✗
discounts received		
– omitted/understated in plca	✔	✗
– omitted/understated in pl	✗	✔
– entered twice/overstated in plca	✗	✔
– entered twice/overstated in pl	✔	✗
other		
– credit balance recorded in error as debit in pl	✔	✗
– debit balance recorded in error as credit in pl	✗	✔

SET-OFF/CONTRA ENTRIES

These entries occur when the same person or business has a subsidiary account in both receivables ledger and payables ledger – ie they are both buying from, and selling to, the business whose accounts we are preparing. For example, Patel Limited has the following accounts in its receivables and payables ledgers:

RECEIVABLES LEDGER

Dr		A Smith		Cr
		£		£
Balance b/d		200		

PAYABLES LEDGER

Dr		A Smith		Cr
		£		£
			Balance b/d	300

From these accounts we can see that:

- A Smith owes Patel Limited £200 (receivables ledger)

- Patel Limited owes A Smith £300 (payables ledger)

To save each having to make a bank payment to the other, it is possible (with A Smith's agreement) to set-off one account against the other, so that they can settle their net indebtedness with one bank payment. The bookkeeping entries in Patel's books will be:

- *debit* A Smith (payables ledger) £200

- *credit* A Smith (receivables ledger) £200

The accounts will now appear as:

RECEIVABLES LEDGER

Dr		A Smith		Cr
		£		£
Balance b/d		200	Set-off: payables ledger	200

PAYABLES LEDGER

Dr		A Smith		Cr
	£			£
Set-off: receivables ledger	200	Balance b/d		300

The net result is that Patel Limited owes A Smith £100. The important point to note is that, because transactions have been recorded in the subsidiary ledger accounts, an entry needs to be made in the two control accounts:

– *debit* payables ledger control account

– *credit* receivables ledger control account

Set-off transactions should be appropriately documented and authorised.

VALUE ADDED TAX (VAT) CONTROL ACCOUNT

the purpose of VAT control account

The purpose of VAT control account is to bring together totals of VAT from books of prime entry, such as the day books and cash book. The diagram on page 63 shows how VAT control account fits into the accounting system.

It is from VAT control account that the VAT Return is prepared, checked and then submitted electronically to HM Revenue & Customs – often quarterly, ie every three months. The VAT Return shows:

■ either, the money amount due to be paid by the business when VAT collected from sales is greater than the VAT paid on purchases

■ or, the money amount due as a refund from HM Revenue & Customs to the business when VAT collected from sales is less than the VAT paid on purchases

verifying VAT control account

Whilst VAT control account does not have subsidiary accounts in receivables or payables ledger to reconcile against, it is nevertheless a totals account. The VAT amounts must be recorded from the books of prime entry; the balance of VAT control account tells the business how much is due to or from HM Revenue & Customs. The account balance must be verified with the amount shown on the business VAT Return – any discrepancy should be investigated immediately and the error(s) traced.

VAT control account explained

A typical layout of a VAT control account with sample figures is shown below. Study the layout carefully and then read the text which follows.

Dr		VAT control account		Cr
	£			£
Purchases	30,000	Sales		40,000
Sales returns	1,500	Purchases returns		1,000
Discounts allowed	200	Discounts received		100
Cash purchases	4,000	Cash sales		5,000
Other cash expenses	500	Other cash income		200
Balance c/d	10,100			
	46,300			46,300
		Balance b/d		10,100

purchases

The amount of VAT from the totals row of purchases day book, being the VAT paid by the business on its credit purchases.

sales returns

The amount of VAT from the totals row of sales returns day book, being the VAT allowed back to customers of the business on the sales returns they make.

discounts allowed

The amount of VAT from the totals row of discounts allowed day book, being the VAT on credit notes issued to customers in respect of prompt payment discount.

cash purchases and other cash expenses

The total of the VAT column from the payments side of cash book, and also petty cash book, is debited to VAT control account. This total comprises VAT paid on the cash purchases of the business, including other expenses – both capital and revenue – paid for as cash transactions.

sales

The amount of VAT from the totals row of sales day book, being the VAT calculated by the business on its credit sales.

continued on page 64

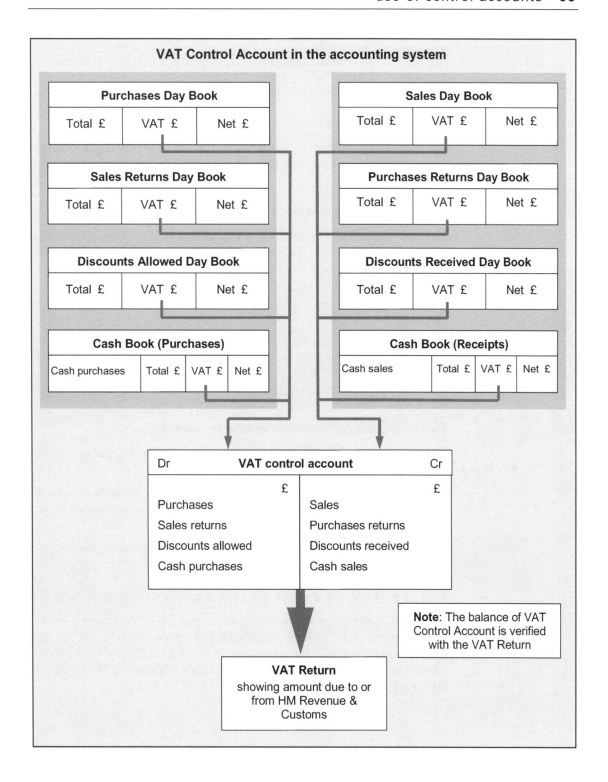

VAT Control Account in the accounting system

Purchases Day Book		
Total £	VAT £	Net £

Sales Day Book		
Total £	VAT £	Net £

Sales Returns Day Book		
Total £	VAT £	Net £

Purchases Returns Day Book		
Total £	VAT £	Net £

Discounts Allowed Day Book		
Total £	VAT £	Net £

Discounts Received Day Book		
Total £	VAT £	Net £

Cash Book (Purchases)			
Cash purchases	Total £	VAT £	Net £

Cash Book (Receipts)			
Cash sales	Total £	VAT £	Net £

Dr	VAT control account	Cr
	£	£
Purchases	Sales	
Sales returns	Purchases returns	
Discounts allowed	Discounts received	
Cash purchases	Cash sales	

Note: The balance of VAT Control Account is verified with the VAT Return

VAT Return
showing amount due to or from HM Revenue & Customs

purchases returns

The amount of VAT from the totals row of purchases returns day book, being the VAT allowed back to the business by its suppliers on purchases returns.

discounts received

The amount of VAT from the totals row of discounts received day book, being the VAT on credit notes received from suppliers in respect of prompt payment discount.

cash sales and other cash income

The total of the VAT column from the receipts side of cash book is credited to VAT control account. This total comprises VAT collected on the cash sales of the business, including other income – both capital and revenue – received as cash transactions.

the journal

Another book of prime entry is the journal, which is discussed in detail in the next chapter. From time to time there may be an entry from the journal to VAT control account. However, this will be for a non-regular transaction.

balance

The balance on VAT control account can be either debit or credit:

- a debit balance brought down indicates that the amount is due as a refund to the business from HM Revenue & Customs

- a credit balance brought down indicates that the amount is due to be paid by the business to HM Revenue & Customs (which is the situation for the majority of businesses)

The balance of the account will be settled with a bank payment either from or to HM Revenue & Customs.

VAT control account in the accounting system

VAT control account is a general ledger account which uses totals from the books of prime entry, including cash book and petty cash book. The account is the source information for preparation of the VAT Return of the business, which is submitted electronically to HM Revenue & Customs. The balance of VAT control account must be verified with the VAT Return.

CONTROL ACCOUNTS AS AN AID TO MANAGEMENT

instant information

When the manager of a business needs to know the figure for trade receivables, trade payables or VAT – important information for the manager – the balance of the appropriate control account will give the information immediately. There is no need to add up the balances of all the subsidiary customer/supplier accounts, or to go to the books of prime entry for VAT amounts.

With a digital bookkeeping system, the control accounts are easily accessed at any time.

prevention of fraud

The use of control accounts makes fraud more difficult – particularly in a manual accounting system. If a fraudulent transaction is to be recorded on a subsidiary account, the transaction must also be entered in the control account. As the control account will be either maintained by a supervisor, or checked regularly by the manager, the control accounts add another level of security within the accounting system. In most accounting systems, staff are only able to access the accounting information appropriate to their work.

location of errors

Control accounts can also help in locating errors. Remember, though, that a control account only proves the arithmetical accuracy of the accounts which it controls – there could still be errors within the subsidiary ledger section.

limitation of control accounts

Whilst control accounts can help in locating errors, they do have the limitation that not all errors will be shown. For example, if a transaction is entered into the wrong trade receivable's subsidiary account within receivables ledger, this will not be revealed when the control account is reconciled to the subsidiary accounts.

Chapter Summary

- Control accounts (or totals accounts) are 'master' accounts, which control a number of subsidiary (memorandum) accounts.

- Three commonly used control accounts are:
    - receivables ledger control account
    - payables ledger control account
    - Value Added Tax control account

- Transactions are recorded on the same side of the control account as on the subsidiary accounts.

- Set-off/contra entries occur when the same person or business has a subsidiary account in both receivables ledger and payables ledger, and it is agreed to set-off one balance against the other to leave a net balance. This usually results in the following control account entries:
    - *debit* payables ledger control account
    - *credit* receivables ledger control account

- In most accounting systems, control accounts are incorporated into the general ledger of the double-entry bookkeeping system. The subsidiary accounts are in separate ledgers – receivables ledger and payables ledger.

- At regular intervals control accounts are reconciled as follows:
    - receivables ledger control account to the total of the balances of the subsidiary accounts in receivables ledger
    - payables ledger control account to the total of the balances of the subsidiary accounts in payables ledger
    - VAT control account to the amount due to or from HM Revenue & Customs

- Control accounts are an aid to management:
    - they give instant information on the total of trade receivables/trade payables/VAT
    - they make fraud more difficult
    - they help to locate errors (but not all errors will be shown)

Key Terms	**control account**	a 'master' account which controls a number of subsidiary (memorandum) accounts
	receivables ledger control account	the general ledger account which controls the receivables ledger
	payables ledger control account	the general ledger account which controls the payables ledger
	Value Added Tax control account	the general ledger account which brings together totals of VAT from the books of prime entry
	set-off/contra entries	where balances in the receivables ledger and the payables ledger are set-off against one another
	aged trade receivables/payables analysis	a summary of each customer/supplier balance analysed into columns showing how long the amounts have been outstanding

Activities

4.1 You have the following information:

- opening customer balances at start of month £18,600
- credit sales for month £9,100
- sales returns for month £800
- money received from customers for month £7,800

What is the figure for closing customer balances at the end of the month? Tick the correct option.

(a)	£2,500	
(b)	£19,100	
(c)	£19,900	
(d)	£20,700	

4.2 Prepare a receivables ledger control account for the month of June 20-7 from the following information:

20-7		£
1 Jun	Debit balance brought down	17,491
30 Jun	Credit sales for month	42,591
	Sales returns from credit customers	1,045
	Money received from credit customers	39,024

Balance the account at 30 June 20-7.

4.3 You work as an accounts assistant for Shire Traders. Today you are working on the receivables ledger control account and receivables ledger.

A summary of transactions with credit customers during June 20-5 is shown below.

	£
Goods sold on credit	118,600
Money received from credit customers	96,214
Discounts allowed	300
Goods returned by credit customers	650
Irrecoverable debt written off	350

The balance of customer accounts at 1 June 20-5 was £180,824.

(a)   Prepare a receivables ledger control account for the month of June 20-5 from the above details. Show clearly the balance carried down at 30 June 20-5.

Receivables ledger control account

Date 20-5	Details	Amount £	Date 20-5	Details	Amount £

The following subsidiary account balances were in the receivables ledger on 30 June 20-5:

	£	
Carless and Company	76,560	debit
BBT Limited	28,109	debit
Dale and Company	32,019	debit
Vale Computers	1,645	debit
Brandon Limited	350	debit
Bissell and Bradley	31,304	debit
Hopkins and Company	32,273	debit

(b)   Reconcile these balances with the receivables ledger control account balance you calculated in (a).

	£
Receivables ledger control account balance as at 30 June 20-5	....
Total of receivables ledger accounts as at 30 June 20-5	....
Difference	....

(c)   What may have caused the difference calculated in (b)?

....

....

....

4.4 You work as an accounts assistant for Southtown Supplies. Today you are working on the receivables ledger control account and receivables ledger.

A summary of transactions with credit customers in September 20-2 is shown below.

(a) Show with a tick whether each entry will be a debit or credit in the receivables ledger control account in the general ledger.

	Amount £	Debit	Credit
Balance of credit customers at 1 September 20-2	47,238		
Goods sold to credit customers	31,054		
Money received from credit customers	29,179		
Goods returned by credit customers	2,684		
Discounts allowed	784		
Irrecoverable debt written off	450		

(b) What will be the balance of credit customers on 1 October 20-2 on the above account? Tick the correct option.

(a)	£44,295	
(b)	£45,195	
(c)	£45,645	
(d)	£46,095	

(c) The balances in the receivables ledger on 1 October 20-2 totalled £44,728.

What is the difference between the total of the balances in the receivables ledger and the receivables ledger control account balance calculated in part (b)?

£
Workings:

(d) Identify the **two** reasons, either of which might have caused the difference.

(a)	Discounts allowed has been understated in the receivables ledger	
(b)	Goods returned have been understated in the receivables ledger	
(c)	The irrecoverable debt written off has been omitted from the receivables ledger	
(d)	Money received from customers has been overstated in the receivables ledger	
(e)	Sales to credit customers have been overstated in the receivables ledger	
(f)	Sales to credit customers have been understated in the receivables ledger	
(g)	Trade discounts have not been included in the receivables ledger	

4.5 You work as an accounts assistant for Bransford Supplies. Today, 2 April 20-8, you have printed out the aged trade receivables analysis as at 31 March 20-8, as follows:

Bransford Supplies Aged trade receivables analysis at 31 March 20-8				
Customer	Total	0-30 days	31-60 days	61+ days
	£	£	£	£
Benn Ltd	2,430	630	1,800	0
Charteris & Co	1,760	1,760	0	0
D Morgan	940	820	120	0
Wilson & Sons	3,610	0	0	3,610
Totals	8,740	3,210	1,920	3,610

The trade terms of Bransford Supplies are 'net 30 days'.

For each of the customer accounts listed, indicate the action you suggest should be taken by the accounts supervisor.

	No action	Letter/email	Letter/email + phone call
Benn Ltd			
Charteris & Co			
D Morgan			
Wilson & Sons			

4.6 You have the following information:

- opening supplier balances at start of month   £15,300
- credit purchases for month   £8,100
- purchases returns for month   £200
- payments made to credit suppliers   £15,800

What is the figure for closing supplier balances at the end of the month? Tick the correct option.

(a)	£7,000	
(b)	£7,400	
(c)	£23,200	
(d)	£23,600	

4.7 Prepare a payables ledger control account for the month of April 20-9 from the following information:

20-9		£
1 Apr	Credit balance brought down	14,275
30 Apr	Credit purchases for month	36,592
	Purchases returns to credit suppliers	653
	Payments made to credit suppliers	31,074
	Contra entry (set-off against receivables ledger control account)	597

Balance the account as at 30 April 20-9.

4.8 You work as an accounts assistant for Durning Traders. Today you are working on the payables ledger control account and payables ledger.

A summary of transactions with credit suppliers during May 20-3 is shown below.

	£
Goods purchased on credit	21,587
Payments made to credit suppliers	13,750
Discounts received	500
Goods returned to credit suppliers	250

The balance of suppliers at 1 May 20-3 was £50,300.

(a) Prepare a payables ledger control account for the month of May 20-3 from the above details. Show clearly the balance carried down at 31 May 20-3.

Payables ledger control account

Date 20-3	Details	Amount £	Date 20-3	Details	Amount £

(b)   The following subsidiary account balances were in the payables ledger on 31 May 20-3:

Wright and Company	£12,000	credit
CCY Limited	£11,107	credit
Carter and Company	£9,380	credit
Tomkins Limited	£16,800	credit
PP Properties	£500	debit
L Vakas	£1,200	credit
Ten Traders	£6,400	credit

Reconcile these balances with the payables ledger control account balance you calculated in (a).

	£
Payables ledger control account balance as at 31 May 20-3	....
Total of payables ledger accounts as at 31 May 20-3	....
Difference	....

(c)   What may have caused the difference calculated in (b)?

....

....

....

4.9   You work as an accounts assistant for Mawla Supplies. Today you are working on the payables ledger control account and payables ledger.

A summary of transactions with credit suppliers during August 20-4 is shown below.

(a)   Show whether each entry will be a debit or credit in the payables ledger control account in the general ledger.

	Amount £	Debit	Credit
Balance of credit suppliers at 1 August 20-4	46,297		
Purchases from credit suppliers	22,084		
Payments made to credit suppliers	25,934		
Discounts received	425		
Goods returned to credit suppliers	1,108		

(b)   What will be the balance of credit suppliers on 1 September 20-4 on the above account? Tick the correct option.

(a)	£41,764	
(b)	£48,614	
(c)	£43,130	
(d)	£40,914	

(c)   The following credit balances were in the payables ledger on 1 September 20-4.

	£
Perran Ltd	5,340
Chiverton & Co	2,195
Durning Builders	11,084
Chapelporth Ltd	7,319
Sennen & Co	3,107
Zelah plc	10,861

Reconcile the balances shown above with the payables ledger control account balance calculated in part (b).

	£
Balance on payables ledger control account at 1 September 20-4	
Total of the payables ledger balances at 1 September 20-4	
Difference	

(d) Which **one** of the following errors may have caused the difference calculated in part (c)?

(a)	An invoice was entered twice in the payables ledger	
(b)	A credit note was not entered in the payables ledger	
(c)	A credit note was entered twice in the payables ledger control account	
(d)	A credit note was not entered in the payables ledger control account	

4.10 Indicate whether the following will be recorded as debits or credits in VAT control account:

	Debit	Credit
VAT on credit purchases		
VAT on cash sales		
VAT on purchases returns		
VAT on credit sales		
VAT on sales returns		
VAT on discounts allowed		
VAT on discounts received		

4.11   You work as an accounts assistant for Blenheim Builders. Today you are working on the VAT control account.

The following figures have been taken from Blenheim Builders' books of prime entry for the three months ended 30 June 20-4:

Sales day book	
Net	£56,000
VAT	£11,200
Total	£67,200

Purchases day book	
Net	£23,200
VAT	£4,640
Total	£27,840

Sales returns day book	
Net	£1,440
VAT	£288
Total	£1,728

Purchases returns day book	
Net	£1,120
VAT	£224
Total	£1,344

Cash book: cash sales	
Net	£2,480
VAT	£496
Total	£2,976

(a)   From the books of prime entry, record the entries in the VAT control account of Blenheim Builders for the three months ended 30 June 20-4.

VAT control account

Date 20-4	Details	Amount £	Date 20-4	Details	Amount £

(b)   Balance VAT control account at 30 June 20-4 and show the balance brought down on 1 July 20-4.

(c)   The VAT Return calculation has been completed by another accounts assistant and shows an amount owing to HM Revenue & Customs of £7,280.

Is the VAT Return correct? | Yes / No |

If it is not correct, what do you think has caused the error?

5 The journal

this chapter covers...

The journal is the book of prime entry for non-regular accounting transactions. Like other books of prime entry – eg sales day book – the purpose of the journal is to list transactions before they are recorded in the double-entry bookkeeping system.

In this chapter we will see how the journal is used to record non-regular transactions such as:

■ *opening entries (the first transactions to open the accounts of a new business)*

■ *irrecoverable debt write off (where a customer's account is to be written off)*

■ *payroll transactions (the accounting entries which record wages and salaries paid to employees)*

A further purpose of the journal is to show the entries required to correct errors found in the accounting system. The topic of correction of errors is covered in Chapter 7.

PURPOSE OF THE JOURNAL

The journal completes the accounting system by providing the book of prime entry for non-regular transactions which are not recorded in any other book of prime entry. Such non-regular transactions include:

- opening entries for a new business
- irrecoverable debts written off
- payroll transactions
- correction of errors (see Chapter 7)

The purposes of the journal are:

- to provide a book of prime entry for non-regular transactions
- to eliminate the need for remembering why non-regular transactions were recorded in the accounts – the journal acts as a record
- to reduce the risk of fraud, by making it difficult for unauthorised transactions to be recorded in the accounting system
- to reduce the risk of errors, by listing the transactions that are to be recorded in the double-entry accounts
- to ensure that entries can be traced back to an authorised financial document (note that documentation is stored securely for possible future reference)

THE JOURNAL – A BOOK OF PRIME ENTRY

The journal is a book of prime entry; it is not part of the double-entry bookkeeping system. The journal lists the transactions that are to be recorded in the general ledger accounts. The accounting system for non-regular transactions is as follows:

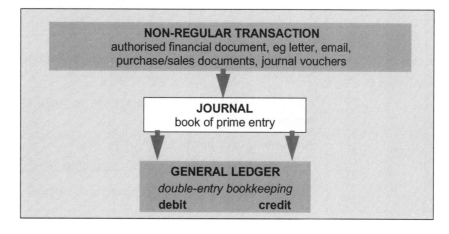

The journal is set out in the following way, with a sample transaction:

Date	Details	Reference	Dr	Cr
20-4			£	£
1 Jul	Bank	CB	20,000	
	Capital	GL		20,000
	Opening capital introduced			

Notes:

■ journal entries are prepared from authorised financial documents (which are stored securely for possible future reference)

■ the names of the accounts to be debited and credited in the accounting system are shown in the details column; it is customary to list the debit transaction first

■ the money amount of each debit and credit entry is stated in the appropriate column

■ the reference column shows where each account is found (eg CB = Cash Book, GL = General Ledger)

■ a journal entry always balances, ie debit and credit entries are for the same amount or total

■ it is usual to include a brief narrative (ie a few words) explaining why the transaction is being carried out, and making reference to the financial document whenever possible (you should always include a narrative unless specifically told otherwise)

■ each journal entry is complete in itself and is separate from the next entry

Note that any transactions involving receivables ledger control account and payables ledger control account must also be recorded in the subsidiary accounts in receivables ledger and payables ledger respectively.

OPENING ENTRIES FOR A NEW BUSINESS

Opening entries are the transactions to open the accounts of a new business.

An example of an opening entry is:

1 Jan 20-4 Started in business with £10,000 in the bank

This non-regular transaction is entered in the journal as follows:

Date	Details	Reference	Dr	Cr
20-4			£	£
1 Jan	Bank	CB	10,000	
	Capital	GL		10,000
	Opening capital introduced			

After the journal entry has been made, the transaction is recorded in the double-entry accounts, as follows:

GENERAL LEDGER

Dr					**Cash Book**			Cr
20-4	**Details**	**Cash**	**Bank**	**20-4**	**Details**	**Cash**	**Bank**
		£	£			£	£
1 Jan	Capital		10,000				

Dr		**Capital account**		Cr
20-4		£	20-4	£
			1 Jan Bank	10,000

Here is another opening entries transaction for a new business to be recorded in the journal:

1 Feb 20-4   *Started in business with cash £100, bank £5,000, inventory £1,000, machinery £2,500, trade payables £850*

The journal entry is:

Date	Details	Reference	Dr	Cr
20-4			£	£
1 Feb	Cash	CB	100	
	Bank	CB	5,000	
	Inventory	GL	1,000	
	Machinery	GL	2,500	
	Payables ledger control	GL		850
	Capital*	GL		7,750
			8,600	8,600
	Assets and liabilities			
	at the start of business			

*Assets – liabilities = capital (ie 100 + 5,000 + 1,000 + 2,500 – 850 = 7,750)

Notes:

- capital is, in this example, the balancing figure, ie assets minus liabilities

- the journal is the book of prime entry for all opening entries for a new business, including cash and bank; however, the normal book of prime entry for other cash/bank transactions is the cash book

- the amounts for the journal entry will now need to be recorded in the general ledger accounts as follows:

GENERAL LEDGER

Dr					Cash Book			Cr
20-4	**Details**	**Cash**	**Bank**	**20-4**	**Details**	**Cash**	**Bank**
		£	£			£	£
1 Feb	Capital	100	5,000				

Dr		Inventory account		Cr
20-4		£	20-4	£
1 Feb	Capital	1,000		

Dr		Machinery account		Cr
20-4		£	20-4	£
1 Feb	Capital	2,500		

Dr		Payables ledger control account		Cr
20-4		£	20-4	£
			1 Feb Capital	850

Dr		Capital account		Cr
20-4		£	20-4	£
			1 Feb Journal	7,750

■ the individual amounts making up the £850 recorded in payables ledger control account must be recorded in the subsidiary accounts in payables ledger

■ the cross-reference in capital account is to the journal – in this way it is possible to refer back to the journal entry to see the assets and liabilities which formed the opening capital of the business. Alternatively, individual amounts of the opening assets and liabilities could be recorded in capital account and cross-referenced with the name of their general ledger account.

IRRECOVERABLE DEBTS WRITTEN OFF

An irrecoverable debt is a debt owing to a business which it considers will never be paid.

One of the problems of selling goods and services on credit terms is that, from time to time, some trade receivables will not pay. As a consequence, the balances of such trade receivables' accounts have to be written off when they become irrecoverable (uncollectable). This happens when all efforts to recover the amounts owing have been exhausted – ie statements, emails and letters have been sent to the customer requesting payment, and legal action (where appropriate) or the threat of legal action, has failed to obtain payment.

In writing off a trade receivable's account as irrecoverable, the business is bearing the cost of the amount due. The account is written off and the amount is debited to irrecoverable debts written off account.

Towards the financial year-end, it is good practice for the accounts supervisor (or other authorised person) to go through the trade receivables' accounts to see if any need to be written off. The accounts supervisor will then advise the accounts assistant which accounts are to be written off (the advice – often in the form of an email – forms the prime document for the irrecoverable debt write off).

We have already seen, in Chapter 4, the double-entry bookkeeping entries to write off a trade receivable's account:

– *debit* irrecoverable debts account

– *debit* Value Added Tax account (if appropriate)

– *credit* receivables ledger control account (and credit the subsidiary account of the customer in receivables ledger)

For example:

15 Dec 20-4   *The accounts supervisor emails you telling you to write off the account of Don's Diner, which has a balance of £48 (including VAT) on 1 December 20-4, as an irrecoverable debt*

The journal entry is:

Date	Details	Reference	Dr	Cr
20-4			£	£
15 Dec	Irrecoverable debts	GL	40	
	Value Added Tax	GL	*8	
	Receivables ledger control	GL		48
			48	48
	Balance of subsidiary receivables ledger account of Don's Diner written off as an irrecoverable debt, as per email from accounts supervisor			

*with VAT at 20 per cent, the VAT amount is one-sixth of the total figure

After the journal entry has been made, the transaction is recorded in the general ledger accounts as follows:

GENERAL LEDGER

Dr			Irrecoverable debts account			Cr
20-4			£	20-4		£
15 Dec	Receivables ledger control		40			

Dr			Value added tax account			Cr
20-4			£	20-4		£
15 Dec	Receivables ledger control		8			

Dr			Receivables ledger control account			Cr
20-4			£	20-4		£
				15 Dec	Irrecoverable debts	40
				15 Dec	Value Added Tax	8

In receivables ledger, the subsidiary account of Don's Diner is recorded as follows:

RECEIVABLES LEDGER

Dr			Don's Diner			Cr
20-4			£	20-4		£
1 Dec	Balance b/d		48	15 Dec	Irrecoverable debts	40
				15 Dec	Value Added Tax	8
			48			48

With the irrecoverable debt written off, this account now has a nil balance.

PAYROLL TRANSACTIONS

what is meant by payroll transactions?

Payroll transactions are the accounting entries which record wages and salaries paid to employees.

Payroll transactions require journal and accounting entries for:

– gross pay

– net pay

– income tax (PAYE – Pay As You Earn)

– employer's National Insurance contributions

– employees' National Insurance contributions

– employer's pension contributions

– employees' pension contributions

– voluntary deductions from employees' pay

what payroll transactions are entered in the accounts?

The payroll transactions to be entered into the accounts are:

- **gross pay**, which is the amount of employees' pay before any deductions

- **net pay**, which is the amount paid to employees after deductions for income tax, employees' National Insurance contributions, employees' pension fund contributions and voluntary deductions

- **income tax (PAYE)** collected by the employer and paid to HM Revenue & Customs

- **employer's National Insurance** contributions paid to HM Revenue & Customs

- **employees' National Insurance** contributions collected by the employer and paid to the HM Revenue & Customs

- **pension contributions provided by the employer** and paid to pension funds

- **employees' pension contributions** deducted from employees' pay and paid to pension funds

- **voluntary deductions**, eg trade union fees, deducted from employees' pay and paid to the organisation

accounts used in payroll transactions

The double-entry accounts used to record payroll transactions are:

bank

This records:

- payment of the net pay of employees
- payment to outside agencies – the deductions to HM Revenue & Customs, payments to pension funds, and payments for voluntary deductions

wages control account

This is the main account for payroll. All transactions for payroll pass through this account which forms one half of the double-entry – a debit or credit to wages control account will be a credit or debit in one of the other payroll accounts

wages expense

This is the employer's expense account for paying employees, which records:

- employees' gross pay
- employer's National Insurance Contributions
- employer's pension contributions

HM Revenue & Customs

This records amounts payable to HM Revenue & Customs for income tax and National Insurance contributions

pension fund

This records amounts payable to external pension funds: the employer's and employees' contributions

wages control account

The diagram on the next page shows the relationship between wages control account and the other payroll accounts. Note that the bank account is not shown here – it is involved in many of the transactions, as we will see in the Case Study on page 88.

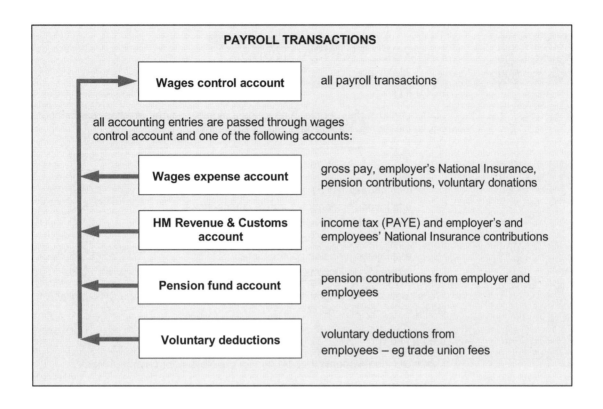

journal and ledger entries

Payroll transactions must be recorded by means of a journal entry in order to be able to trace the accounting entries from the payroll records (the financial document), through the book of prime entry (the journal to the general ledger accounts).

As payroll is quite complex, it is best to take a step-by-step approach (which is used in the Case Study on the next page). The journal entries and ledger entries are as follows:

1   Record the wages expense (the total cost to the employer)

2   Record the net pay (to be paid to employees)

3   Record the liability to HM Revenue & Customs (for income tax and National Insurance contributions)

4   Record the liability to the pension fund (both employer and employee contributions)

5   Record the liability for voluntary deductions, eg trade union fees

The Case Study which follows illustrates this step-by-step approach.

<table>
<tr><td>**Case Study**</td></tr>
</table>

PAYROLL TRANSACTIONS

situation

Matrix employs four people. It operates a monthly payroll which is run on the last day of the month. Payroll amounts for November 20-8 are:

gross pay	£5,500
net pay	£3,820
income tax (PAYE)	£900
employer's National Insurance contributions	£550
employees' National Insurance contributions	£450
employer's pension contributions	£275
employees' pension contributions	£275
voluntary deductions: trade union fees	£55

We will now see the journal and general ledger entries for these payroll transactions, taking a step-by-step approach.

solution

These are the payments that are due for the November payroll of Matrix.

payments due to the employees

Gross pay	£5,500	
less		
Income tax	£900	
National Insurance contributions	£450	
Pension contributions	£275	
Trade union fees	£55	
	———	
Net pay due		£3,820

payment due to HM Revenue & Customs

Income tax deducted from pay	£900	
Employer's National Insurance contributions	£550	
Employees' National Insurance contributions	£450	
	———	
		£1,900

payment due to the pension fund

Employer's contributions	£275	
Employees' contributions, deducted from pay	£275	
	———	
		£550

payment due to voluntary deductions

Employees' payment, for trade union fees, deducted from pay	£55
	———

payments total (wages expense)   £6,325

The four amounts, shown in the right-hand column on the previous page, are recorded in the journal and entered into the general ledger accounts. This is done as follows:

Step 1

Transfer the total of the payments (here £6,325) to wages account (this is the cost to the employer) and to wages control account.

Journal

Date	Details	Reference	Dr	Cr
20-8			£	£
30 Nov	Wages expense	GL	6,325	
	Wages control	GL		6,325
	Transfer of wages expense			

Dr		Wages expense account		Cr
20-8		£	20-8	£
30 Nov	Wages control	6,325		

Dr		Wages control account		Cr
20-8		£	20-8	£
			30 Nov Wages expense	6,325

Note: this total agrees with the payments total of £6,325 (shown on the previous page) which is the total payroll expense to the business for the month.

Step 2

Make entries for the payment of wages (the net pay paid from the bank).

Journal

Date	Details	Reference	Dr	Cr
20-8			£	£
30 Nov	Wages control	GL	3,820	
	Bank	CB		3,820
	Net wages paid to employees			

Dr	Wages control account		Cr
20-8	£	20-8	£
30 Nov Bank	3,820	30 Nov Wages expense	6,325

Dr	Bank account		Cr
20-8	£	20-8	£
		30 Nov Wages control	3,820

Step 3

Transfer the amount due to HM Revenue & Customs to HM Revenue & Customs account.

Journal

Date	Details	Reference	Dr	Cr
20-8			£	£
30 Nov	Wages control	GL	1,900	
	HM Revenue & Customs	GL		1,900
	Amount due to HM Revenue & Customs			

The amount due is £1,900 and comprises income tax £900 and National Insurance contributions – employer's £550 and employees' £450. These amounts may be shown individually in the journal entry and the accounts.

Dr	Wages control account		Cr
20-8	£	20-8	£
30 Nov Bank	3,820	30 Nov Wages expense	6,325
30 Nov HM Revenue & Customs	1,900		

Dr	HM Revenue & Customs account		Cr
20-8	£	20-8	£
		30 Nov Wages control	1,900

Note: This account shows HM Revenue & Customs as a payable of the business. The liability will be paid by the business (*debit* HM Revenue & Customs, *credit* bank) when payment is made to HM Revenue & Customs during the next month.

Step 4

Transfer the amount due to the pension fund.

The amount due is £550 – employer's contribution £275, employees' contribution £275.

Journal

Date	Details	Reference	Dr	Cr
20-8			£	£
30 Nov	Wages control	GL	550	
	Pension fund	GL		550
	Amount due to pension fund			

Dr		**Wages control account**				Cr
20-8			£	20-8		£
30 Nov	Bank		3,820	30 Nov	Wages expense	6,325
30 Nov	HM Revenue & Customs		1,900			
30 Nov	Pension fund		550			

Dr		**Pension fund account**			Cr
20-8		£	20-8		£
			30 Nov	Wages control	550

Note: This account shows the pension fund as a payable of the business. The liability will be paid by the business (*debit* pension fund, *credit* bank) when payment is made to the pension fund provider during the next month.

Step 5

Transfer the amount due for voluntary deductions.

The amount due is £55, being the trade union fees.

Journal

Date	Details	Reference	Dr	Cr
20-8			£	£
30 Nov	Wages control	GL	55	
	Trade union fees	GL		55
	Amount due for trade union fees			

Dr	Wages control account			Cr
20-8		£	20-8	£
30 Nov Bank		3,820	30 Nov Wages expense	6,325
30 Nov HM Revenue				
& Customs		1,900		
30 Nov Pension fund		550		
30 Nov Trade union fees		55		
		6,325		6,325

Dr	Trade Union fees account			Cr
20-8		£	20-8	£
			30 Nov Wages control	55

Note: This account shows trade union fees as a payable of the business. The liability will be paid by the business (*debit* trade union fees, *credit* bank) when payment is made to the trade union during the next month.

conclusion

You will see from the journal and accounting entries shown above that the wages control account records all the payroll accounting transactions carried out each time the payroll is run. At the end of the process, the control account balance reverts to zero. You will see above that the total of both sides after Step 5 transfer is £6,325 – ie the balance is nil.

MAKING JOURNAL ENTRIES

As we have seen in this chapter, the journal is the book of prime entry for non-regular transactions. Because of the irregular nature of journal transactions, it is important that they are correctly authorised by the appropriate person – such as the accounts supervisor, the administration manager, the owner of the business. The authorisation will, ideally, be a financial document – eg letter, email or other document – but may well be verbal – eg "write-off the account of Zelah Limited as an irrecoverable debt".

It is good practice to ensure that journal entries are checked by an appropriate person before they are entered into the general ledger accounts. It is all too easy to get a journal entry the wrong way round, resulting in an error.

In Chapter 7 we will look at the use of the journal when correcting errors in the accounting system.

Chapter Summary

- The journal is used to record non-regular transactions.

- The journal is a book of prime entry – it is not a double-entry account.

- Journal entries are prepared from authorised financial documents, which are stored securely for possible future reference.

- The journal records entries for:
  - opening entries for a new business
  - irrecoverable debts written off
  - payroll transactions
  - correction of errors (see Chapter 7)

- Payroll transactions require journal and accounting entries for:
  - gross pay
  - net pay
  - income tax
  - employer's and employees' National Insurance contributions
  - employer's and employees' pension contributions
  - voluntary deductions from employees' pay

Key Terms

journal	the book of prime entry for non-regular transactions
opening entries	the transactions to open the accounts of a new business
irrecoverable debt written off	a debt owing to a business which it considers will never be paid
payroll transactions	the accounting entries which record wages and salaries paid to employees
wages control account	the main account for payroll through which all transactions for payroll pass
gross pay	the amount of employees' pay before any deductions
net pay	the amount paid to employees after deductions for income tax, employees' National Insurance contributions, employees' pension fund contributions, and voluntary deductions
HM Revenue & Customs	receives amounts from payroll in respect of income tax, employer's National Insurance contributions, and employees' National Insurance contributions

Activities

5.1 Hussain Limited is a furniture manufacturer. Which **one** of the following transactions will be recorded in the journal? Tick the correct option.

(a)	Sale of furniture on credit to a customer	
(b)	Cash purchase of fabric for chair seat covers	
(c)	Write off of a trade receivable's account from receivables ledger as an irrecoverable debt	
(d)	Petty cash purchase of postage stamps	

5.2 Which **one** of the following will not be recorded in the journal? Tick the correct option.

(a)	Payroll transactions	
(b)	Cash sale of goods	
(c)	Write off of an irrecoverable debt	
(d)	Opening entries	

5.3 Which financial transaction goes with which book of prime entry?

Financial transaction

- opening entries for a new business
- credit purchase of goods from a supplier
- returned credit purchases to the supplier
- customer returns goods sold on credit
- BACS credit from a customer
- credit sale of goods to a customer
- expense paid out of petty cash

Book of prime entry

- petty cash book
- sales day book
- purchases day book
- sales returns day book
- purchases returns day book
- journal
- cash book

5.4   Lucy Wallis started in business on 1 May 20-8 with the following assets and liabilities:

	£
Vehicle	6,500
Fixtures and fittings	2,800
Inventory	4,100
Bank	150
Loan from husband	5,000

You are to prepare Lucy's opening journal entry, showing clearly her capital at 1 May 20-8.

5.5   Jane Seymour is setting up a new business and has listed all the accounts and their amounts that will be used. She asks you to complete the journal entry by ticking the appropriate column in the table below, and to calculate her opening capital.

Account name	Amount £	Debit	Credit
Cash	200		
Cash at bank	2,340		
Capital			
Trade payables	3,985		
Trade receivables	4,751		
Loan from bank	12,650		
Office equipment	4,120		
Rent paid	950		
Inventory	2,310		
Sundry expenses	1,194		
Vehicles	8,350		
Wages	2,294		
Journal to record the opening entries of the new business			

5.6   You are an accounts assistant at Baxter Limited. The accounts supervisor has sent you an email instructing you to write off as an irrecoverable debt the account of Boughton and Company, a trade receivable who owes £240 plus VAT at 20%. Which one of the following sets of transactions will you make in the general ledger? Tick the correct option.

(a)	Debit irrecoverable debts £288; credit VAT £48; credit receivables ledger control £240	
(b)	Debit receivables ledger control £288; credit irrecoverable debts £288	
(c)	Debit irrecoverable debts £240; debit VAT £48; credit bank £288	
(d)	Debit irrecoverable debts £240; debit VAT £48; credit receivables ledger control £288	

5.7   You are employed by Tyax Trading as an accounts assistant. Today the accounts supervisor sends you the following email:

EMAIL
To   accountsassistant@tyax.co.uk
From   accountssupervisor@tyax.co.uk
Subject   Receivables Ledger: Smithers and Sons
The above credit customer has ceased trading, owing us £840 plus VAT at 20%. Please record the journal entries needed in general ledger to write off as an irrecoverable debt the net amount and the VAT. Use the layout below and account names from the list.

Account name	Amount £	Debit	Credit

Select your account names from the following list: Irrecoverable debts, Payables ledger control, Purchases, Receivables ledger control, Sales, Smithers and Sons, Tyax Trading, Value Added Tax.

The following information is used in multiple-choice questions 5.8 to 5.10. In each case, choose one option from (a) to (d).

The payroll system of Home Fires Limited has recorded the following totals for the month of July:

gross pay	£350,780
income tax	£69,500
employer's National Insurance contributions	£35,085
employees' National Insurance contributions	£31,450
employer's pension contributions	£7,500
employees' pension contributions	£7,500
trade union fees	£1,500

5.8   The total payment to HM Revenue & Customs for the month is:

(a)	£100,950	
(b)	£104,585	
(c)	£15,000	
(d)	£136,035	

5.9   The total wages expense to the employer is:

(a)	£350,780	
(b)	£462,865	
(c)	£393,365	
(d)	£308,195	

5.10   The total net pay to employees is:

(a)	£240,830	
(b)	£248,330	
(c)	£388,230	
(d)	£349,280	

5.11   Pegasus Limited has recorded the following payroll totals for the month of October 20-3:

gross pay	£101,500
income tax	£20,500
employer's National Insurance contributions	£10,150
employees' National Insurance contributions	£9,860
trade union fees	£850

You are to:

(a)   Calculate the wages expense.

(b)   Calculate the payment due to HM Revenue & Customs.

(c)   Calculate the net pay due to employees.

(d)   Show the journal entries needed to record:

- the wages expense

- the liability to HM Revenue & Customs

- the net wages paid to employees

- the liability for trade union fees

Select your account names from the following list: Bank, Employees' National Insurance, Employer's National Insurance, HM Revenue & Customs, Income tax, Net wages, Trade Union fees, Wages control, Wages expense.

Wages expense

Account name	Amount £	Debit	Credit

Liability to HM Revenue & Customs

Account name	Amount £	Debit	Credit

Net wages paid to employees

Account name	Amount £	Debit	Credit

Liability for Trade Union fees

Account name	Amount £	Debit	Credit

5.12   Jason's Hotel has recorded the following payroll totals for the month of January 20-5:

gross pay	£50,000
income tax	£11,110
employer's National Insurance contributions	£5,010
employees' National Insurance contributions	£4,985
employer's pension contributions	£1,100
employees' pension contributions	£1,100

Show the journal entries to record:

(a)   the wages expense

(b)   the liability to HM Revenue & Customs

(c)   the net wages paid to the employees

(d)   the liability to the pension fund

Select your account names from the following list: Bank, Employees' National Insurance, Employer's National Insurance, HM Revenue & Customs, Income tax, Net wages, Pension fund, Wages control, Wages expense.

(a)

Account name	Amount £	Debit	Credit

(b)

Account name	Amount £	Debit	Credit

(c)

Account name	Amount £	Debit	Credit

(d)

Account name	Amount £	Debit	Credit

5.13   Identify which **two** of the following situations are a correct use of the journal.

Situation	
Harry is setting up a new business. He is starting with capital of £20,000, a vehicle valued at £8,000 and cash in the bank of £12,000.	
Mandy is seeking a bank loan for her business and, to impress the bank, wishes to process a journal entry for an extra £5,000 of capital which she hopes to put in at the beginning of next year.	
Tara has calculated the figures for next month's payroll. She asks if she can process the transactions through the journal.	
Tomasz, the bookkeeper, is going on holiday. He wants to make a journal entry of notes for the person who is covering the bookkeeping for him.	

5.14 A journal entry for payroll transactions is as follows:

31 July 20-5			Journal number: 101
Account	**Debit**	**Credit**	**Description**
	£	**£**	
Wages expense	25,632		Gross pay
Bank		21,409	Net pay
Wages expense	1,876		Employer's NIC*
HMRC		1,876	Employer's NIC
HMRC		1,732	Employees' NIC
HMRC		2,491	Income tax (PAYE)

* National Insurance Contributions

Prior to this journal entry, the balance of the HM Revenue & Customs account was debit £125.

Show the transactions to be recorded on the HM Revenue & Customs account, calculate the balance carried down after these entries, and total both sides of the account (dates are not required).

HM Revenue & Customs			
Details	**£**	**Details**	**£**
Balance b/d	125		

6 The trial balance

this chapter covers...

The trial balance lists the balances of every account from general ledger, distinguishing between those accounts which have debit balances and those which have credit balances.

The debit balances and credit balances are totalled and, when the two totals are the same, this proves that the accounting records are arithmetically correct.

This chapter shows how to prepare a trial balance manually. When a digital bookkeeping system is in use, a display or printout of the trial balance will be available – in which case, the totals should agree.

A trial balance does not prove the complete accuracy of the accounting system and there may well be errors. Correction of errors is covered in Chapter 7.

EXTRACTING AN INITIAL TRIAL BALANCE

An initial trial balance is extracted from the accounting system for the purpose of making an initial check of the arithmetical accuracy of the double-entry bookkeeping – ie that the debit entries equal the credit entries.

A trial balance is a list of the balances of every account from general ledger (including cash book and petty cash book), distinguishing between those accounts which have debit balances and those which have credit balances, and totalled to show that debits equal credits.

A trial balance is extracted at regular intervals – often at the end of each month – and the balances are set out in two totalled columns, a debit column and a credit column. The debit and credit columns are totalled and the totals should agree. In this way the trial balance proves that the accounting records are arithmetically correct. However, a trial balance does not prove the complete accuracy of the accounting records as there may well be errors – which we will look at in Chapter 7.

An example of a trial balance is shown below.

Trial balance of Ace Suppliers as at 31 January 20-4		
	Dr	Cr
	£	£
Name of account		
Purchases	7,500	
Sales		16,000
Sales returns	250	
Purchases returns		500
Receivables ledger control	1,550	
Payables ledger control		900
Rent	1,000	
Wages	1,500	
Heating and lighting	1,250	
Office equipment	5,000	
Machinery	7,500	
Inventory at 1 Jan 20-4	2,500	
Petty cash	200	
Bank (cash at bank)	4,850	
Value Added Tax		1,200
J Williams: loan		7,000
Capital		10,000
Drawings	2,500	
	35,600	35,600

Note that the order of accounts in the trial balance could be set out:

– in alphabetical order, or

– in numerical order, or

– in random order (as on the previous page), or

– in the order of the financial statements – that is, income and expenditure items from the statement of profit or loss, followed by asset, liability and capital items from the statement of financial position

a note about the asset of inventory

We have seen in earlier studies how businesses use separate purchases and sales accounts to record when the goods in which they trade are bought and sold. The reason for using separate accounts for purchases and sales is because there is usually a difference between the buying price and the selling price – the latter is higher and gives the business its profit. At least once a year, however, a business values the inventory it has on the shelves of the shop, for example, or in the warehouse. As inventory is an asset of a business, the valuation is recorded as a debit to inventory account. This means that there will – for most businesses – be a debit balance on inventory account representing the value of inventory held at the beginning of the financial year. This balance will continue until such time as the inventory is formally valued again – often at the end of the financial year.

The debit balance for inventory is shown in the trial balance, as seen above.

DEBIT AND CREDIT BALANCES – GUIDELINES

Certain accounts always have a debit balance, while others always have a credit balance. The lists set out below act as a guide, and will also help in your understanding of the initial trial balance.

debit balances

Debit balances are assets and expenses, and include:

■ purchases account

■ sales returns account

■ non-current asset accounts, eg premises, motor vehicles, machinery, office equipment, etc

■ inventory account – the inventory valuation, usually at the beginning of the year

■ expenses accounts, eg wages, telephone, rent paid, discount allowed

■ drawings account

- receivables ledger control account (which records the total balances of trade receivables)

- petty cash account

- cash account

credit balances

Credit balances are liabilities, income and capital, and include:

- sales account

- purchases returns account

- income accounts, eg rent received, commission received, fees received, discount received

- capital account

- loan account

- payables ledger control account (which records the total balances of trade payables)

Notes:

- **Bank account** can be either debit or credit – it will be:
  - debit when the business has money in the bank
  - credit when it is overdrawn

- **Value Added Tax account** can be either debit or credit – it will be:
  - debit when VAT is due to the business
  - credit when the business owes VAT to HM Revenue & Customs

IF THE INITIAL TRIAL BALANCE DOESN'T BALANCE

If the initial trial balance fails to balance – ie the two totals are different – there is an error (or errors):

- either in the addition of the trial balance

- and/or in the double-entry bookkeeping

how to find an error

The procedure for finding the error(s) is as follows:

- check the addition of the trial balance

- check that the balance of each account has been correctly entered in the trial balance, and under the correct heading, ie debit or credit

- check that the balance of every account in general ledger has been included in the trial balance, together with the balance of cash book and petty cash book

- check that analysis columns from the cash book (for VAT), and from the petty cash book (for VAT and expenses) have been entered to the general ledger accounts

- check the calculation of the balance on each account

- calculate the amount by which the trial balance is wrong, and then look in the accounts for a transaction for this amount: if one is found, check that the double-entry bookkeeping has been carried out correctly

- halve the amount by which the trial balance is wrong, and look for a transaction for this amount: if it is found, check the double-entry bookkeeping

- if the amount by which the trial balance is wrong is divisible by nine, then the error may be a reversal of figures, eg £65 entered as £56, or £45 entered as £54

- if the trial balance is wrong by a round amount – eg £10, £100, £1,000 – the error is likely to be in the calculation of the account balances

- if the error is still not found, it is necessary to check the bookkeeping transactions since the date of the last trial balance, by going back to the financial documents and books of prime entry

The accounts supervisor needs to be informed if the trial balance still does not balance; he or she will give guidance as to what is to be done.

The Case Study that follows shows how an initial trial balance is constructed from a list of account balances.

INITIAL TRIAL BALANCE

situation

You work as an accounts assistant for Severn Valley Stationery. The company sells office products and equipment to businesses in its area.

Today the accounts supervisor has asked you to work on preparing an initial trial balance as at 30 April 20-4. The supervisor has given you the following list of balances to be transferred to the trial balance.

You are to place the figures in the debit or credit column, as appropriate, and to total the debit and credit columns.

Account name	Amount £	Debit £	Credit £
Vehicles	20,500		
Inventory	11,945		
Bank (overdraft)	8,297		
Petty cash	110		
Receivables ledger control	28,368		
Payables ledger control	12,591		
VAT owing to HM Revenue & Customs	2,084		
Capital	23,237		
Loan from bank	20,500		
Sales	84,837		
Sales returns	1,089		
Purchases	51,054		
Purchases returns	2,210		
Discount allowed	105		
Discount received	215		
Vehicle expenses	3,175		
Wages	22,864		
Rent and rates	8,210		
Advertising	2,174		
Heating and lighting	968		
Travel costs	1,476		
Telephone	732		
Postages	591		
Miscellaneous expenses	610		
Totals	–		

solution

You take each balance in turn and enter it in either the debit balance column or the credit balance column.

You use the following guidelines:

DEBIT BALANCES (to go in the debit column)	CREDIT BALANCES (to go in the credit column)
• purchases	• sales
• sales returns	• purchases returns
• expenses (including discount allowed)	• income (including discount received)
• inventory	• capital
• receivables ledger control	• payables ledger control
• VAT (when refund is due from HM Revenue & Customs)	• VAT (when owed to HM Revenue & Customs)
• bank (cash at bank)	• bank (overdraft)
• cash	• loan/bank loan
• petty cash	
• non-current assets	
• drawings	

When you have entered the balances in the appropriate column, you then total the two columns of the trial balance. If the debit and credit totals are the same, this proves that the accounting records are arithmetically correct. If the trial balance doesn't balance, you follow the procedures for finding error(s) along the lines of those set out on pages 105-106.

The initial trial balance of Severn Valley Stationery as at 30 April 20-4 then appears as shown on the next page.

Account name	Amount £	Debit £	Credit £
Vehicles	20,500	20,500	
Inventory	11,945	11,945	
Bank (overdraft)	8,297		8,297
Petty cash	110	110	
Receivables ledger control	28,368	28,368	
Payables ledger control	12,591		12,591
VAT owing to HM Revenue & Customs	2,084		2,084
Capital	23,237		23,237
Loan from bank	20,500		20,500
Sales	84,837		84,837
Sales returns	1,089	1,089	
Purchases	51,054	51,054	
Purchases returns	2,210		2,210
Discount allowed	105	105	
Discount received	215		215
Vehicle expenses	3,175	3,175	
Wages	22,864	22,864	
Rent and rates	8,210	8,210	
Advertising	2,174	2,174	
Heating and lighting	968	968	
Travel costs	1,476	1,476	
Telephone	732	732	
Postages	591	591	
Miscellaneous expenses	610	610	
Totals	−	153,971	153,971

Note that the format of the initial trial balance shown above includes the original 'Amount' column to show you the process of transferring the account balances to the correct debit or credit column. In reality, the initial trial balance is likely only to show the debit and credit money columns. It will also be headed up with the name of the business and the date of the trial balance.

The trial balance of Severn Valley Stationery is shown in its final form on the next page.

Severn Valley Stationery

Trial Balance as at 30 April 20-4

Account name	Debit	Credit
	£	£
Vehicles	20,500	
Inventory	11,945	
Bank (overdraft)		8,297
Petty cash	110	
Receivables ledger control	28,368	
Payables ledger control		12,591
VAT owing to HM Revenue & Customs		2,084
Capital		23,237
Loan from bank		20,500
Sales		84,837
Sales returns	1,089	
Purchases	51,054	
Purchases returns		2,210
Discount allowed	105	
Discount received		215
Vehicle expenses	3,175	
Wages	22,864	
Rent and rates	8,210	
Advertising	2,174	
Heating and lighting	968	
Travel costs	1,476	
Telephone	732	
Postages	591	
Miscellaneous expenses	610	
Totals	153,971	153,971

TAKING THE TRIAL BALANCE FURTHER

A trial balance is usually the starting point for a further stage in the accounting system – that is, the production of financial statements. These comprise:

- the statement of profit or loss, which shows the profitability, or otherwise, of the business for a particular time period

- the statement of financial position, which shows the assets, liabilities and capital of the business at a particular date

You will study these financial statements in later AAT Units, but awareness of them will help in your current areas of study.

Chapter Summary	▪ Taking the balance of each account in the general ledger, an initial trial balance can be extracted.
	▪ In the initial trial balance, the totals for debit balances and credit balances should be the same.
	▪ If the initial trial balance fails to balance, there is an error (or errors):
	– either in the addition of the trial balance
	– and/or in the double-entry bookkeeping
	▪ The steps for finding an error should be followed.
	▪ The accounts supervisor needs to be informed if the trial balance still does not balance.
	▪ A trial balance does not prove the complete accuracy of the accounting records and there may well be errors that must be corrected.
	▪ A trial balance is usually the starting point for the production of financial statements – the statement of profit or loss, and the statement of financial position.

Key Terms	**trial balance**	list of the balances of every account from general ledger (including cash book and petty cash book), distinguishing between those accounts which have debit balances and those which have credit balances, and totalled to show that debits equal credits
	debit balances	are assets and expenses
	credit balances	are liabilities, income and capital

Activities

6.1 Which **one** of the following accounts always has a debit balance?

(a)	Capital account	
(b)	Purchases account	
(c)	Sales account	
(d)	Purchases returns account	

6.2 Which **one** of the following accounts always has a credit balance?

(a)	Sales returns account	
(b)	Premises account	
(c)	Capital account	
(d)	Wages account	

6.3 Prepare the initial trial balance of Jane Greenwell as at 31 March 20-9, from the following list of balances:

	£
Bank (overdraft)	1,250
Purchases	850
Petty cash	48
Sales	1,940
Purchases returns	144
Payables ledger control	1,442
Equipment	2,704
Van	3,200
Inventory at 1 April 20-8	1,210
Sales returns	90
Receivables ledger control	1,174
Wages	1,500
Capital	6,000

6.4 You work as an accounts assistant for Pershore Products. The accounts supervisor has asked you to work on preparing an initial trial balance as at 30 June 20-2. The supervisor has given you the following list of balances to be transferred to the trial balance.

You are to place the figures in the debit or credit column, as appropriate, and total the debit and credit columns.

Account name	Amount £	Debit £	Credit £
Office equipment	12,246		
Bank (cash at bank)	3,091		
Petty cash	84		
Inventory	11,310		
Capital	22,823		
Drawings	2,550		
VAT owing to HM Revenue & Customs	3,105		
Loan from bank	8,290		
Payables ledger control	17,386		
Receivables ledger control	30,274		
Sales	82,410		
Purchases	39,496		
Purchases returns	2,216		
Sales returns	3,471		
Discounts received	298		
Discounts allowed	517		
Wages	20,212		
Advertising	4,390		
Insurance	1,045		
Heating and lighting	1,237		
Rent and rates	4,076		
Travel costs	854		
Postages	721		
Telephone	954		
Totals	–		

6.5 You work as an accounts assistant for Arley Limited. The accounts supervisor has asked you to work on preparing an initial trial balance as at 31 December 20-6. The supervisor has given you the following list of balances to be transferred to the trial balance.

You are to place the figures in the debit or credit column, as appropriate, and total the debit and credit columns.

Account name	Amount £	Debit £	Credit £
Sales	101,269		
Sales returns	3,476		
Purchases	54,822		
Purchases returns	4,107		
Receivables ledger control	25,624		
Payables ledger control	18,792		
Discounts received	399		
Discounts allowed	210		
Rent and rates	3,985		
Advertising	4,867		
Insurance	1,733		
Wages	31,246		
Heating and lighting	3,085		
Postages	1,211		
Telephone	985		
Travel costs	2,311		
Miscellaneous expenses	107		
Capital	22,489		
Vehicles	22,400		
Inventory	12,454		
Petty cash	85		
Bank (overdraft)	6,291		
VAT owing to HM Revenue & Customs	3,054		
Loan from bank	12,200		
Totals	−		

6.6 You are an accounts assistant at Boxgrove Stores.

Most of the ledger accounts have been closed off and the balances included in the trial balance at 31 July 20-6.

(a) **You are to** complete the remaining ledger accounts by inserting the balance carried down on each account. Enter your answers to two decimal places.

Bank

20-6	Details	£	20-6	Details	£
1 Jul	Balance b/d	2,054.61	20 Jul	Stationery	1,201.45
6 Jul	Sales	3,109.18	25 Jul	Purchases	5,298.51
31 Jul	Receivables ledger control	12,506.87	31 Jul	Payables ledger control	14,309.28
31 Jul	Balance c/d				

Discounts received

20-6	Details	£	20-6	Details	£
			1 Jul	Balance b/d	1,245.39
			31 Jul	Payables ledger control	98.76
31 July	Balance c/d				

Receivables ledger control

20-6	Details	£	20-6	Details	£
1 Jul	Balance b/d	24,510.64	31 Jul	Bank	12,506.87
14 Jul	Sales	7,385.96			
28 Jul	Sales	3,225.68	31 Jul	Balance c/d	

VAT control

20-6	Details	£	20-6	Details	£
31 Jul	Purchases	2,966.39	1 Jul	Balance b/d	1,805.92
			31 Jul	Sales	2,286.80
31 Jul	Balance c/d				

(b) Complete the trial balance by inserting the missing figures and calculating the totals for each column. Enter your answers to two decimal places.

Item	Debit £	Credit £
Sales		61,406.53
Purchases	43,286.03	
Bank		
Discounts received		
Business rates	3,104.21	
Stationery	2,768.33	
Payables ledger control		4,758.39
Receivables ledger control		
VAT control		
Totals		

7 Correction of errors

this chapter covers...

As we have seen in the previous chapter, a trial balance does not prove the complete accuracy of the accounting records and there may well be errors.

Errors fall into two groups:

- *errors not disclosed by the trial balance*
- *errors disclosed by the trial balance*

In this chapter, we look at the types of errors within each of these groups and, when they are found, we explain how to correct them using journal entries. We also see how the trial balance is redrafted following adjustments.

ERRORS IN THE ACCOUNTING SYSTEM

In any accounting system, there is always the possibility of errors – both in the books of prime entry and in the ledgers. As noted in the previous chapter, a trial balance does not prove the complete accuracy of the accounting records and there may well be errors.

Ways to avoid errors, or ways to reveal them sooner, include:

- division of the accounting function between a number of people, so that no one person is responsible for all aspects of a business transaction
- statements of account issued regularly to customers, who will check the transactions on their accounts and advise of any discrepancies
- checking of statements of account received from suppliers against the accounting records
- extraction of a trial balance at regular intervals
- checking of bank statements and preparing bank reconciliation statements
- checking cash and petty cash balances against cash held
- the use of control accounts
- the use of a digital bookkeeping system

Despite all of these precautions, errors will still occur from time to time.

We will look at:

- correction of errors not shown by a trial balance
- correction of errors shown by a trial balance, using a suspense account

We look at each of these two groups and see the journal entry needed to correct the various types of errors, together with the ledger entries and the effect on the trial balance.

ERRORS NOT DISCLOSED BY THE TRIAL BALANCE

A trial balance does not prove the complete accuracy of the accounting records.

There are six types of errors that are not disclosed by the trial balance, as follows:

error of omission

Here, a financial transaction has been completely omitted from the accounting records – ie both the debit and credit entries have not been made.

error of commission

Here, a transaction is entered to the wrong person's account. For example, a sale of goods on credit to T Hughes has been entered as debit to J Hughes' account. Double-entry bookkeeping has been completed and the receivables ledger control account will reconcile with the receivables ledger. However, when J Hughes receives a statement of account, he or she will soon complain about being debited with goods not ordered or received.

An error of commission can also occur between other accounts, such as expenses or non-current assets.

error of principle

This is when a transaction has been entered in the wrong type of account. For example, the cost of fuel for vehicles has been entered as debit vehicles account, credit bank account. The error is that vehicles account is a non-current asset, and the transaction should have been debited to the expense account for vehicle running expenses. If not corrected, such an error of principle will show a false financial position for the business.

error of original entry

Here, the correct accounts have been used, and the correct sides: what is wrong is that the amount has been entered incorrectly in both accounts. This could be caused by a 'bad figure' on an invoice or a cheque, or it could be caused by a 'reversal of figures', eg an amount of £45 being entered in both accounts as £54. Note that both debit and credit entries need to be made incorrectly for the trial balance still to balance; if one entry has been made incorrectly and the other is correct, then the error will be shown.

reversal of entries

With this error, the debit and credit entries have been made in the accounts but on the wrong side of the two accounts concerned. For example, a cash sale has been entered wrongly as debit sales account, credit cash account. (This should be entered as debit cash account, credit sales account.)

compensating error

Here, two errors cancel each other out. For example, if the balance of purchases account is calculated wrongly at £10 too much, and a similar error has occurred in calculating the balance of sales account, then the two errors will compensate each other, and the trial balance will not show the errors.

Although these errors are not shown by a trial balance, they are likely to come to light if the procedures suggested on the previous page are followed. For example, a customer will soon let you know if their account has been debited with goods they did not buy.

When an error is found, it needs to be corrected by means of a journal entry which shows the correcting bookkeeping entries. Remember that all journal entries are prepared from authorised financial documents. These could take the form of an email or a note from the accounts supervisor; such documents, together with any other paperwork, should be stored securely for possible future reference.

A practical hint which may help in correcting errors is to write out the double-entry accounts as they appear with the error; then write in the correcting entries and see if the result has achieved what was intended.

ERRORS NOT DISCLOSED BY THE TRIAL BALANCE: JOURNAL ENTRIES

We will now see the errors which are not disclosed by the trial balance and show an example journal entry for each. Remember that:

- the journal is the book of prime entry for non-regular transactions

- journal entries must be recorded in the general ledger accounts

- for journal entries which involve receivables ledger control account or payables ledger control account, the transactions must also be recorded in the accounts in the subsidiary ledger – either receivables ledger or payables ledger

For each example error, the correcting journal and ledger entries are shown.

error of omission

Credit sale of goods, £200 plus VAT (at 20%) on invoice 4967 to H Jarvis completely omitted from the accounting system; the error is corrected on 12 May 20-4.

Date	Details	Reference	Dr	Cr
20-4			£	£
12 May	Receivables ledger control	GL	240	
	Sales	GL		200
	VAT	GL		40
			240	240
	Invoice 4967 omitted from accounts: in the receivables ledger – debit H Jarvis £240			

GENERAL LEDGER

Dr   **Receivables ledger control account**   Cr

20-4	£	20-4	£
12 May Sales/VAT	240		

Dr   **Sales account**   Cr

20-4	£	20-4		£
		12 May	Receivables ledger control	200

Dr   **Value added tax account**   Cr

20-4	£	20-4		£
		12 May	Receivables ledger control	40

RECEIVABLES LEDGER

Dr   **H Jarvis**   Cr

20-4	£	20-4	£
12 May Sales/VAT	240		

An error of omission can happen in a very small business – often where the bookkeeping is done by one person: for example, an invoice is 'lost' down the back of a filing cabinet. Where documents are numbered in sequence, then none should be mislaid.

error of commission

Credit sales of £48, including VAT (at 20%) on invoice no 321 have been debited to the account of J Adams, instead of the account of J Adams Limited; the error is corrected on 17 May 20-4.

Date	Details	Reference	Dr	Cr
20-4			£	£
17 May	Receivables ledger control	GL	48	
	Receivables ledger control	GL		48
	Correction of error (invoice 321): in the receivables *ledger – debit J Adams Limited £48 – credit J Adams £48*			

GENERAL LEDGER

Dr	Receivables ledger control account			Cr
20-4		£	20-4	£
17 May Receivables ledger control		48	17 May Receivables ledger control	48

RECEIVABLES LEDGER

Dr	J Adams Limited			Cr
20-4		£	20-4	£
17 May J Adams		48		

Dr	J Adams			Cr
20-4		£	20-4	£
			17 May J Adams Limited	48

An error of commission can be avoided, to some extent, by the use of account numbers, and by persuading the customer to quote the account number or reference on each transaction. All digital bookkeeping systems use numbers/references to identify accounts, but it is still possible to post a transaction to the wrong account.

An error of commission can also occur between other accounts, such as expenses or non-current assets. For example, if an expense for advertising has been debited in error to administrative expenses account, this will need to be corrected through a journal entry and the two accounts involved.

error of principle

The cost of fuel, £50 (excluding VAT) on receipt no 34535, has been debited to vehicles account; the error is corrected on 20 May 20-4.

Date	Details	Reference	Dr	Cr
20-4			£	£
20 May	Vehicle expenses	GL	50	
	Vehicles	GL		50
	Correction of error: *receipt 34535*			

GENERAL LEDGER

Dr	Vehicle expenses account			Cr
20-4		£	20-4	£
20 May Vehicles		50		

Dr			Vehicles account			Cr
20-4		£	20-4			£
			20 May	Vehicle expenses		50

An error of principle is similar to an error of commission except that, instead of the wrong person's account being used, it is the wrong class of account.

In the above example, the vehicle running costs must be kept separate from the cost of the asset (the vehicle), otherwise the expense and asset accounts will be incorrect, leading to the ledger accounts showing a false financial position for the business.

error of original entry

Postages of £45 paid from the bank entered in the accounts as £54; the error is corrected on 27 May 20-4.

Do not correct an error like this by putting an amount for the difference through the accounts – here by debiting bank and crediting postages with £9. The reason for saying this is that there was no original transaction for this amount. Instead we must make two journal entries to:

- remove the incorrect entry

- record the correct entry

In this example, the journal entries are:

Date	Details	Reference	Dr	Cr
20-4			£	£
27 May	Bank	CB	54	
	Postages	GL		54
	Removing the incorrect entry:			
	transaction entered as £54			
	instead of £45			

Date	Details	Reference	Dr	Cr
20-4			£	£
27 May	Postages	GL	45	
	Bank	CB		45
	Recording the correct entry:			
	transaction entered as £54			
	instead of £45			

GENERAL LEDGER

Dr	Cash book (bank columns)			Cr
20-4	£	20-4		£
27 May Postages	54	27 May Postages		45

Dr	Postages account			Cr
20-4	£	20-4		£
27 May Bank	45	27 May Bank		54

A reversal of figures either has a difference of nine (as above), or an amount divisible by nine. An error of original entry can also be a 'bad' figure on a cheque, an invoice or a credit note, entered wrongly into both accounts.

reversal of entries

A bank payment, on 3 May 20-4 for £50 to a trade payable, S Wright, has been debited in the cash book and credited to payables ledger control account; this is corrected on 12 May 20-4.

This error can be corrected with a single journal entry for £100 (debit payables ledger control, credit bank) – you may see this in AAT Assessments. Alternatively, two journal entries can be made to:

▪ remove the incorrect entry

▪ record the correct entry

The two journal entries are:

Date	Details	Reference	Dr	Cr
20-4			£	£
12 May	Payables ledger control	GL	50	
	Bank	CB		50
	Removing the incorrect entry (bank payment): in the payables ledger debit S Wright £50			

Date	Details	Reference	Dr	Cr
20-4			£	£
12 May	Payables ledger control	GL	50	
	Bank	CB		50
	Recording the correct entry (bank payment): in the payables ledger debit S Wright £50			

It is often an idea to write out the accounts, complete with the error, and then to write in the correcting entries. The two accounts involved in this last error are shown with the error made on 3 May, and the corrections made on 12 May indicated by the shading:

GENERAL LEDGER

Dr			Payables ledger control account			Cr
20-4		£	20-4			£
12 May	Bank	50	3 May	Bank		50
12 May	Bank	50				

Dr			Cash book (bank columns)			Cr
20-4		£	20-4			£
3 May	S Wright	50	12 May	S Wright		50
			12 May	S Wright		50

The accounts now show a net debit transaction of £50 on payables ledger control account, and a net credit transaction of £50 on bank account, which is how this payment to a supplier should have been recorded in the first place.

compensating error

Rent paid account is overcast (ie it is over-added) by £100; sales account is also overcast by the same amount; the error is corrected on 31 May 20-4.

Date	Details	Reference	Dr	Cr
20-4			£	£
31 May	Sales	GL	100	
	Rent paid	GL		100
	Correction of overcast on rent paid account and sales account			

GENERAL LEDGER

Dr	Sales account			Cr
20-4	£	20-4		£
31 May Rent paid	100			

Dr	Rent paid account			Cr
20-4	£	20-4		£
		31 May Sales		100

In this example, an account with a debit balance – rent paid – has been overcast; this is compensated by an overcast on an account with a credit balance – sales. There are several permutations on this theme, eg two debit balances, one overcast, one undercast; a debit balance undercast, a credit balance undercast.

TRIAL BALANCE ERRORS: USE OF SUSPENSE ACCOUNT

There are six types of errors which are disclosed by the trial balance:

- calculation errors in ledger accounts
- single entry transactions
- recording two debits or two credits for a transaction
- recording different amounts for the debit and credit entries
- errors in transferring balances to the trial balance
- omission of a general ledger account in the trial balance

When errors are disclosed, the initial trial balance is 'balanced' by creating a journal entry for the difference and opening a suspense account, as shown in the Case Study below.

Case Study

SUSPENSE ACCOUNT

situation

The accounts assistant of Temeside Traders is unable to balance the initial trial balance on 31 December 20-4. As the error or errors cannot be found quickly, the trial balance is balanced by creating a journal entry for the difference and opening a suspense account:

	Dr	Cr
	£	£
Trial balance totals	100,000	99,700
Suspense account		300
	100,000	100,000

solution

A journal entry is created to open a suspense account with, in this case, a credit balance of £300:

Date	Details	Reference	Dr	Cr
20-4			£	£
31 Dec	Suspense	GL		300
	Trial balance difference as at 31 December 20-4			

The suspense account is opened in general ledger as follows:

GENERAL LEDGER

Dr	**Suspense account**		Cr
20-4	£	20-4	£
		31 Dec Trial balance difference	300

A detailed examination of the bookkeeping system is now made in order to find the errors. As errors are found, they are corrected by means of a journal entry. The journal entries balance, with one part of the entry being either a debit or credit to suspense account. In this way, the balance on suspense account is eliminated by bookkeeping transactions.

In the next section, we discuss how errors which are disclosed by the trial balance are corrected and see an example journal entry for each.

ERRORS DISCLOSED BY THE TRIAL BALANCE: JOURNAL ENTRIES

We now look at the journal entries needed to correct errors which are disclosed by the trial balance and present an example for each.

At the end of this section we see how the suspense account from the Case Study above appears after the errors have been found and corrected on 4 January 20-5.

calculation errors in ledger accounts and books of prime entry

Sales account was undercast (under-added) by £100 on 23 December 20-4.

As sales account was undercast, the correcting entry must credit sales account with £100. The correcting journal entry and ledger entry are:

Date	Details	Reference	Dr	Cr
20-5			£	£
4 Jan	Suspense	GL	100	
	Sales	GL		100
	Undercast on 23 December 20-4 now corrected			

GENERAL LEDGER

Dr		Sales account		Cr
20-5		£	20-5	£
			4 Jan Suspense	100

The entry in suspense account is shown on page 133.

Note: calculation errors can also occur in the books of prime entry, ie sales day book, purchases day book, etc.

single entry transactions

Telephone expenses of £55 were not recorded in the expenses account on 10 December 20-4.

As only the bank entry has been recorded, the correcting entry must complete double-entry bookkeeping by debiting telephone expenses account with £55. The correcting journal entry and ledger entry are:

Date	Details	Reference	Dr	Cr
20-5			£	£
4 Jan	Telephone expenses	GL	55	
	Suspense	GL		55
	Omission of entry in expenses account: bank payment on 10 December 20-4			

GENERAL LEDGER

Dr		Telephone expenses account		Cr
20-5		£	20-5	£
4 Jan Suspense		55		

The entry in suspense account is shown on page 133.

recording two debits or two credits for a transaction

Stationery expenses of £48 were debited to both stationery account and bank account on 18 December 20-4.

As bank account has been debited in error with £48, the correcting journal entry can be in two parts to:

▪ remove the incorrect entry

▪ record the correct entry

Date	Details	Reference	Dr	Cr
20-5			£	£
4 Jan	Suspense	GL	48	
	Bank	CB		48
	Removing the incorrect entry: payment for stationery expenses debited to bank in error on 18 December 20-4			

Date	Details	Reference	Dr	Cr
20-5			£	£
4 Jan	Suspense	GL	48	
	Bank	CB		48
	Recording the correct entry: payment for stationery expenses debited to bank in error on 18 December 20-4			

GENERAL LEDGER

Dr	Cash book (bank columns)		Cr
20-5	£	20-5	£
		4 Jan Suspense	48
		4 Jan Suspense	48

The entries in suspense account are shown on page 133.

Note that an alternative treatment is to record a single journal entry, here for the total of £98 (debit bank, credit suspense) – you may see this in AAT assessments.

recording different amounts for debit and credit entries

Payment made to A Wilson, a supplier, for £65 has been entered in bank account as £56 on 19 December 20-4.

As the credit entry in bank account has been entered incorrectly, the correcting journal entry can be in two parts to:

▪ remove the incorrect entry

▪ record the correct entry

Date	Details	Reference	Dr	Cr
20-5			£	£
4 Jan	Bank	CB	56	
	Suspense	GL		56
	Removing the incorrect entry: payment to a supplier entered in bank account as £56 instead of £65 on 19 December 20-4			

Date	Details	Reference	Dr	Cr
20-5			£	£
4 Jan	Suspense	GL	65	
	Bank	CB		65
	Recording the correct entry: payment to a supplier entered in bank account as £56 instead of £65 on 19 December 20-4			

GENERAL LEDGER

Dr	Cash Book (bank columns)		Cr
20-5	£	20-5	£
4 Jan Suspense	56	4 Jan Suspense	65

The entries in suspense account are shown on page 133.

Note that an alternative treatment is to record a single journal entry, here for the net amount of £9 (debit suspense, credit bank) – you may see this in AAT Assessments.

errors in transferring balances to the trial balance

The balance of rent account is £11,100 but it has been recorded in the trial balance as £11,000.

To correct this type of error needs a journal entry to take the wrong amount from suspense account and then to record the correct amount, ie a two-part journal entry. As rent account has a debit balance, the journal entries are firstly to take out the wrong balance (debit suspense account and credit rent account in the trial balance) and then to record the correct balance (debit rent account in the trial balance and credit suspense account).

Date	Details	Reference	Dr	Cr
20-5			£	£
4 Jan	Suspense	GL	11,000	
	Removing the incorrect balance of rent account from the trial balance as at 31 December 20-4			

Date	Details	Reference	Dr	Cr
20-5			£	£
4 Jan	Suspense	GL		11,100
	Recording the correct balance of rent account in the trial balance as at 31 December 20-4			

Each of these journal entries is for a single transaction; the reason for this is because the account for rent is correct in general ledger and is not affected by the error of recording the wrong amount in the trial balance.

The entries in suspense account are shown on page 133.

Note that some businesses may have a policy of not recording journal entries to correct this type of error. As the ledger account balance is correct, policy might be to amend the incorrect balance and the balance of suspense account directly on the face of the trial balance.

omission of a general ledger account in the trial balance

Discounts received account has been omitted from the trial balance. The balance of the account is £250 credit.

To correct this type of error needs a journal entry to record the balance which has been omitted. As this example omits an account with a credit balance, we must record the inclusion of the account as debit suspense account and credit discount received account in the trial balance.

Date	Details	Reference	Dr	Cr
20-5			£	£
4 Jan	Suspense	GL	250	
	Recording the correct balance of discounts received account in the trial balance as at 31 December 20-4			

This is a single entry transaction in the journal because the omitted account is correct in general ledger and is not affected by its omission in the trial balance. The entry in suspense account is shown below.

Note that some businesses may have a policy of correcting this type of error directly on the face of the trial balance without recording a journal entry.

suspense account

After these journal entries have been recorded in the general ledger accounts, suspense account appears as:

Dr		Suspense account		Cr
20-5	£	20-4		£
4 Jan Sales	100	31 Dec Trial balance difference		300
4 Jan Bank	48	20-5		
4 Jan Bank	48	4 Jan Telephone expenses		55
4 Jan Bank	65	4 Jan Bank		56
4 Jan Rent	11,000	4 Jan Rent		11,100
4 Jan Discounts received	250			
	11,511			11,511

Thus all the errors have been found, and suspense account now has a nil balance.

REDRAFT THE TRIAL BALANCE FOLLOWING ADJUSTMENTS

In the previous section, we have seen how a suspense account is used to 'balance' an initial trial balance. The suspense account can have either a debit or a credit balance – it will depend on which of the columns of the initial trial balance is the lower amount. For example, from the Case Study on pages 127-128, the credit column of the trial balance was £300 less than the debit column: this means that £300 had to be credited to suspense account to 'balance' the trial balance.

Once a suspense account has been opened, it is necessary to locate the errors in the accounting system – we have seen the six types of error that are revealed by a trial balance. When they have been found, the errors are corrected by means of journal entries from which the ledgers are updated. Correcting errors have an effect on the trial balance and it is necessary to redraft the trial balance in order to show:

- that suspense account has been cleared

- the adjusted account balances

The Case Study which follows shows how an initial trial balance is redrafted to clear suspense account and adjust the account balances.

REDRAFT THE TRIAL BALANCE FOLLOWING ADJUSTMENTS

situation

On 30 June 20-6 Beacon Traders prepared an initial trial balance which did not balance, and a suspense account with a credit balance of £720 was opened.

On 1 July journal entries were prepared to correct the errors that had been found, and to clear the suspense account.

The list of balances in the initial trial balance, and the journal entries to correct the errors, are shown on the next page.

As the accounts assistant at Beacon Traders, you are to redraft the trial balance by placing the figures in the debit or credit column. You take into account the journal entries to clear the suspense account.

Account names	Balances extracted on 30 June 20-6 £	Balances at 1 July 20-6	
		Debit £	**Credit £**
Vehicles	20,500		
Inventory	11,945		
Bank (overdraft)	7,847		
Petty cash	110		
Receivables ledger control	28,368		
Payables ledger control	12,591		
VAT owing to HM Revenue & Customs	2,084		
Capital	20,670		
Loan from bank	20,500		
Sales	84,567		
Sales returns	1,089		
Purchases	51,054		
Purchases returns	2,210		
Vehicle expenses	3,175		
Wages	22,864		
Rent and rates	8,210		
Advertising	2,174		
Heating and lighting	968		
Telephone	732		
Suspense account (credit balance)	720		
	Totals		

Journal entries

Account name	Debit £	Credit £
Suspense	225	
Bank		225
Suspense	225	
Bank		225

Account name	Debit £	Credit £
Sales	4,250	
Suspense		4,250
Suspense	4,520	
Sales		4,520

solution

The first thing you do is to check that the journal entries will clear the suspense account. You do this by entering up the suspense account from the journal entries as follows:

Dr		Suspense account		Cr
20-6	£	20-6		£
1 Jul Bank	225	30 Jun Trial balance difference		720
1 Jul Bank	225	1 Jul Sales		4,250
1 Jul Sales	4,520			
	4,970			4,970

Next you amend the account balances affected by the journal entries:

Dr		Bank account		Cr
20-6	£	20-6		£
1 Jul Balance c/d	8,297	30 Jun Balance b/d		7,847
		1 Jul Suspense		225
		1 Jul Suspense		225
	8,297			8,297
		1 Jul Balance b/d		8,297

Dr		Sales account		Cr
20-6	£	20-6		£
1 Jul Suspense	4,250	30 Jun Balance b/d		84,567
1 Jul Balance c/d	84,837	1 Jul Suspense		4,520
	89,087			89,087
		1 Jul Balance b/d		84,837

Lastly you redraft the trial balance, on the next page, which balances without using a suspense account. This shows that the accounting records are now arithmetically correct.

Account names	Balances extracted on 30 June 20-6	Balances at 1 July 20-6	
	£	Debit £	Credit £
Vehicles	20,500	20,500	
Inventory	11,945	11,945	
Bank (overdraft)	7,847		8,297
Petty cash	110	110	
Receivables ledger control	28,368	28,368	
Payables ledger control	12,591		12,591
VAT owing to HM Revenue & Customs	2,084		2,084
Capital	20,670		20,670
Loan from bank	20,500		20,500
Sales	84,567		84,837
Sales returns	1,089	1,089	
Purchases	51,054	51,054	
Purchases returns	2,210		2,210
Vehicle expenses	3,175	3,175	
Wages	22,864	22,864	
Rent and rates	8,210	8,210	
Advertising	2,174	2,174	
Heating and lighting	968	968	
Telephone	732	732	
Suspense account			–
Totals		151,189	151,189

Tutorial note: the accounts affected by the journal entries are bank, sales and suspense.

Chapter Summary

■ A trial balance does not prove the complete accuracy of the accounting records as there may be:

– errors not disclosed by the trial balance

– errors disclosed by the trial balance

■ Errors not disclosed by the trial balance are:

– error of omission

– error of commission

– error of principle

– error of original entry

– reversal of entries

– compensating error

■ Errors disclosed by the trial balance are:

– calculation errors in ledger accounts and books of prime entry

– single entry transactions

– recording two debits or two credits for a transaction

– recording different amounts for the debit and credit entries

– errors in transferring balances to the trial balance

– omission of a general ledger account in the trial balance

■ Correction of errors is always a difficult topic to put into practice: it tests knowledge of double-entry bookkeeping and it is all too easy to make the error worse than it was in the first place! The secret of correcting errors is to write down – in account format – what has gone wrong. It should then be relatively easy to see what has to be done to put the error right.

■ All errors are non-regular transactions and need to be corrected by means of a journal entry: the bookkeeper then records the correcting transactions in the general ledger accounts.

■ When errors are disclosed by the trial balance, the amount of the imbalance is placed in a suspense account. As the errors are found, journal entries are made which 'clear out' the suspense account.

Key Terms	**error of omission**	financial transaction completely omitted from the accounting records
	error of commission	transaction entered to the wrong person's account, or between other accounts, such as expenses or non-current assets
	error of principle	transaction entered in the wrong type of account
	error of original entry	wrong amount entered in accounts
	reversal of entries	debit and credit entries made on the wrong side of the accounts
	compensating error	where two errors cancel each other
	suspense account	account in which is placed the amount of an error shown by the initial trial balance, pending further investigation
	redrafted trial balance	trial balance which has been amended following correction of errors

Activities

7.1 The following errors have been made in the accounting records of Beacon Traders. Tick to show which of the errors below are, or are not, disclosed by the trial balance.

Error in the general ledger	Error disclosed by the trial balance	Error not disclosed by the trial balance
A bank payment for telephone expenses has been recorded on the debit side of both the cash book and telephone expenses account		
A payment recorded in bank account for vehicle repairs has been entered in vehicles account		
A sales invoice has been omitted from all accounting records		
The balance of purchases returns account has been calculated incorrectly		
A bank payment from a trade receivable has been recorded in cash book and receivables ledger only		
A bank payment of £85 for stationery has been recorded as £58 in both accounts		

7.2 An amount has been entered into the accounting system as £65 instead of £56. The error is called:

(a)	Compensating error	
(b)	Error of commission	
(c)	Error of principle	
(d)	Error of original entry	

Which **one** of these options is correct?

7.3 A trial balance failed to balance. The debit column totalled £154,896 and the credit column totalled £155,279. What entry would be made in the suspense account to balance the trial balance? Tick the correct option.

(a)	£766 debit	
(b)	£383 debit	
(c)	£383 credit	
(d)	£766 credit	

7.4 A trial balance fails to agree by £75 and the difference is placed in a suspense account. Later it is found that a cash sale for this amount has not been entered in the sales account. Which one of the following journal entries is correct?

(a)	Debit suspense account £75; credit sales account £75	
(b)	Debit suspense account £150; credit sales account £150	
(c)	Debit sales account £75; credit suspense account £75	
(d)	Credit sales account £75	

7.5 The following errors have been made in the general ledger of Mereford Manufacturing:

(a) £100 has been debited to rent account instead of to business rates account.

(b) Sales returns have been entered into the accounting records as £96 instead of the correct amount of £69.

(c) Purchases returns of £175 have been debited to purchases returns account and credited to payables ledger control account.

(d) Fuel for vehicles of £45 has been debited to vehicles account.

You are to record the journal entries to correct the errors shown above in the general ledger (dates and narratives are not required).

7.6 The trial balance of Thomas Wilson balanced. However, a number of errors have been found in the accounting records:

(a) Credit sale of £150 to J Rigby has not been entered in the accounts.

(b) A bank payment for £125 to H Price Limited, a trade payable, has been recorded in the account of H Prince.

(c) The cost of a new delivery van, £10,000, has been entered to vehicle expenses account.

(d) Postages of £55, paid by bank payment, have been entered on the wrong sides of both accounts.

(e) Both purchases account and purchases returns account have been undercast by £100.

(f) A bank receipt for £89 from L Johnson, a trade receivable, has been entered in the accounts as £98.

You are to take each error in turn and:

• State the type of error

• Show the correcting journal entry

7.7 The trial balance of Rose's Retail included a suspense account. All the bookkeeping errors have now been traced and the journal entries shown below have been recorded.

Journal entries

Account name	Debit £	Credit £
Telephone expenses	210	
Suspense		210
Suspense	100	
Sales		100
Vehicle expenses	50	
Vehicles		50

As the accounts assistant at Rose's Retail, **you are to** enter the journal entries in the general ledger accounts (shown on the next page). Dates are not required.

Select your entries for the details column from the following list: Balance b/f, Sales, Suspense, Telephone expenses, Vehicle expenses, Vehicles.

Telephone expenses account

Details	Amount £	Details	Amount £

Suspense account

Details	Amount £	Details	Amount £
Balance b/d	110		

Sales account

Details	Amount £	Details	Amount £

Vehicle expenses account

Details	Amount £	Details	Amount £

Vehicles account

Details	Amount £	Details	Amount £

7.8 The initial trial balance of Carrick Cards at 30 April 20-1 did not balance. The difference of £100 was placed into a suspense account.

The error has been traced to the sales day book as shown below.

Sales day book

Date 20-1	Details	Invoice number	Total £	VAT £	Net £
30 Apr	Bialas Ltd	4591	2,400	400	2,000
30 Apr	Corline and Co	4592	1,440	240	1,200
30 Apr	Thorpe Traders	4593	960	160	800
	Totals		4,800	700	4,000

(a) As an accounts assistant at Carrick Cards **you are to** identify the error and record the journal entries needed for the general ledger to:

(1) remove the incorrect entry

(2) record the correct entry

(3) remove the suspense account balance

Select your account names, from the following list: Bialas Ltd, Corline and Co, Purchases, Purchases day book, Payables ledger control, Purchases returns, Purchases returns day book, Sales, Sales day book, Receivables ledger control, Sales returns, Sales returns day book, Suspense, Thorpe Traders, Value Added Tax.

(1)

Account name	Amount £	Debit	Credit

(2)

Account name	Amount £	Debit	Credit

(3)

Account name	Amount £	Debit	Credit

(b)   A further error is discovered – a bank payment for vehicle expenses of £89 has been entered in the accounts as £98.

You are to record the journal entries needed for the general ledger to:

(1)   remove the incorrect entry

(2)   record the correct entry

Select your account names from the following list: Bank, Cash, Purchases, Payables ledger control, Sales, Receivables ledger control, Suspense, Value Added Tax, Vehicle expenses.

(1)

Account name	Amount £	Debit	Credit

(2)

Account name	Amount £	Debit	Credit

7.9   Jeremy Johnson extracts a trial balance from his accounting records on 30 September 20-4. Unfortunately the trial balance fails to balance and the difference, £19 debit, is placed to a suspense account pending further investigation.

The following errors are later found:

(a)   A bank payment of £85 for office expenses has been entered in the bank account but no entry has been made in the office expenses account.

(b)   A bank payment for photocopying of £87 has been correctly entered in the bank account, but is shown as £78 in the photocopying account.

(c)   Sales returns account has been overcast by £100.

(d)   Commission received of £25 has been entered twice in the account.

You are to:

•   Make journal entries to correct the errors

•   Show the suspense account after the errors have been corrected

7.10 On 31 December 20-4 Chapelporth Supplies prepared an initial trial balance which did not balance, and a suspense account was opened. On 2 January 20-5 journal entries were prepared to correct the errors that had been found, and to clear the suspense account. The list of balances in the initial trial balance, and the journal entries to correct the errors, are shown on the next page.

As the accounts assistant at Chapelporth Supplies, you are to redraft the trial balance by placing the figures in the debit or credit column. You should take into account the journal entries which will clear the suspense account.

Account names	Balances on 31 December 20-4	Balances at 2 January 20-5	
	£	Debit £	Credit £
Office equipment	12,246		
Bank (cash at bank)	3,091		
Petty cash	84		
Inventory	11,310		
Capital	18,246		
Loan from bank	8,290		
VAT owing to HM Revenue & Customs	3,105		
Payables ledger control	17,386		
Receivables ledger control	30,274		
Sales	82,410		
Purchases	39,996		
Purchases returns	2,216		
Sales returns	3,471		
Wages	20,212		
Advertising	4,300		
Insurance	1,045		
Heating and lighting	1,237		
Rent and business rates	4,076		
Postages	721		
Suspense account (credit balance)	410		
Totals			

Journal entries

Account name	Debit £	Credit £
Suspense	780	
Advertising		780
Advertising	870	
Suspense		870

Account name	Debit £	Credit £
Suspense	5,500	
Purchases		5,500
Purchases	5,000	
Suspense		5,000

7.11 On 30 April 20-8 Towanporth Traders prepared an initial trial balance which did not balance, and a suspense account was opened. On 1 May journal entries were prepared to correct the errors that had been found, and to clear the suspense account. The list of balances in the initial trial balance, and the journal entries to correct the errors, are shown below.

As the accounts assistant at Towanporth Traders, you are to redraft the trial balance by placing the figures in the debit or credit column. You should take into account the journal entries which will clear the suspense account.

Account names	Balances on 30 April 20-8	Balances at 1 May 20-8	
	£	Debit £	Credit £
Sales	101,169		
Sales returns	3,476		
Purchases	54,822		
Purchases returns	4,107		
Receivables ledger control	25,624		
Payables ledger control	18,792		
Rent and rates	3,985		
Advertising	4,867		
Insurance	1,733		
Wages	27,391		
Heating and lighting	3,085		
Miscellaneous expenses	107		
Capital	18,171		
Vehicles	22,400		
Inventory	12,454		
Petty cash	85		
Bank (overdraft)	6,041		
VAT owing to HM Revenue & Customs	3,054		
Loan from bank	12,200		
Suspense account (debit balance)	3,505		
Totals			

Journal entries

Account name	Debit £	Credit £
Suspense	100	
Sales		100

Account name	Debit £	Credit £
Wages	3,855	
Suspense		3,855

Account name	Debit £	Credit £
Suspense	125	
Bank		125
Suspense	125	
Bank		125

7.12 The trial balance of Amy's business has disclosed that there are errors – the amount of the imbalance is placed in a suspense account.

(a) Identify which **two** of the following statements about suspense accounts are true.

Statement	
A suspense account is created when errors are not disclosed by the trial balance.	
A suspense account can have either a debit balance or a credit balance.	
When the debit side total of a trial balance is less than the credit side total, a suspense is opened with a debit balance.	
If the errors cannot be found quickly, the balance of suspense account is written off to irrecoverable debts account.	

(b) Identify whether each of the errors described below would or would not be disclosed by the trial balance.

Error	Disclosed	Not disclosed
Purchases account has been undercast by £1,000.		
Amy used personal cash to pay for fuel for the business van but has forgotten to record the transaction in the accounts.		

7.13 Lyn and Kasia run a retail business. They use a manual accounting system and have prepared a trial balance at the year-end. The trial balance shows total debits of £25,778 and total credits of £27,294.

Lyn and Kasia have identified the following errors:

- Error 1: Rent paid for January 20-2 of £1,525 was credited to bank account but was not recorded in rent paid account.

- Error 2: The day book total of sales for February 20-2 was £1,454. The amount entered in sales account in the general ledger was £1,445.

(a) What is the balance of suspense account in the trial balance?

£ [   ]

This balance is (tick the answer):

Debit	
Credit	

(b) Complete the table below with the account names required to show the debits and credits that will be processed through the journal to clear suspense account.

30 June 20-2	Journal number 49		
Account	**Debit**	**Credit**	**Description**
	£	**£**	
	1,525		Correction of error 1
		1,525	Correction of error 1
	9		Correction of error 2
		9	Correction of error 2

7.14 You are an accounts assistant at Elmhurst Trading. You are asked to redraft a trial balance after some errors have been identified and the correcting journal entries have been made.
The initial list of balances for Elmhurst Trading at 31 March is:

Item	£
Sales	80,392.78
Purchases	52,894.68
Discounts allowed	254.21
Bank	10,886.27
Vehicles	33,610.34
Payables ledger control	14,860.27

The errors have been identified and the following journal entries need to be processed:

Date: 31 March 20-1		Journal number: 065		
Date	Description	Debit £	Credit £	
31 March	Discounts allowed	28.27		Discounts allowed not recorded in discounts allowed account
31 March	Suspense		28.27	Discounts allowed not recorded in discounts allowed account
31 March	Suspense	2,420.72		Sales of £1,210.36 recorded on debit side of sales account
31 March	Sales		2,420.72	Sales of £1,210.36 recorded on debit side of sales account

You are to complete the adjusted trial balance by inserting the correct figures in either the debit or credit column, and calculating the totals for each column.

Item	Debit £	Credit £
Sales		
Purchases		
Discounts allowed		
Bank		
Vehicles		
Payables ledger control		
Totals		

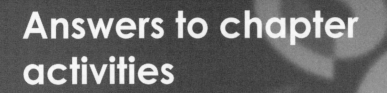

Answers to chapter activities

CHAPTER 1: PAYMENT METHODS

1.1 (a) Small items of office expenditure

(c) The wages of an employee who does not have a bank account

1.2 (a) A written and signed instruction by a customer to their bank to pay a specific amount of money to a named person or business

1.3 (d) is true; (a), (b) and (c) are false

1.4 (c) It can be used for a sales representative who travels for the business and has to pay for expenses incurred

1.5 (a) Are equal in amount

1.6 **(a)** paying variable amounts to twenty suppliers at the end of each month 6

(b) paying a monthly business rates bill of twelve fixed instalments of £258.90 1

(c) buying a new car costing £34,000 for delivery the following day 3

(d) paying an electricity bill which has variable quarterly payments 4

(e) buying a jar of coffee for office use from the local foodstore 2

(f) paying £350,000 to a firm of solicitors for the purchase of a new shop 5

options:

1 standing order

2 cash which you can claim back from the person who operates the petty cash system

3 bank draft

4 direct debit

5 CHAPS payment

6 BACS direct credit

1.7

Description	Payment method
A payment made by card where the amount is reserved immediately in the bank account	Debit card
An instruction in writing signed by the bank's customer telling the bank to pay an amount to a named person	Cheque
An electronic payment for a high value same-day payment	CHAPS
An instruction to the bank to make the same regular payments from the bank account	Standing order

CHAPTER 2: PAYMENT METHODS AND THE BANK ACCOUNT BALANCE

2.1 **(a)** A positive balance on a bank account is called a **credit** balance.

(b) A negative balance on a bank account is called a **debit** balance.

2.2 (a) A bank account should be kept in credit whenever possible

2.3 (a) Cheques should be paid in as soon as possible

2.4 (b) Payments should be made later rather than earlier, but not too late

2.5

		Same day	Next day	Next month
(a)	Debit card		✔	
(b)	Cash	✔		
(c)	CHAPS	✔		
(d)	Credit card			✔
(e)	Faster Payment	✔		

2.6 (a) Tuesday (one working day after Monday)

CHAPTER 3: BANK RECONCILIATION STATEMENTS

3.1 (a) Unpresented cheques

3.2 (a) £100 credit

3.3

TOM REID	
BANK RECONCILIATION STATEMENT AS AT 31 DECEMBER 20-2	
	£
Closing bank statement balance	207
Less: unpresented cheque:	
B Kay (cheque no 345126)	320
	(113)
Add: outstanding lodgement:	
J Hill	13
Closing cash book balance	(100)

3.4 (a)

Cash book (bank columns)

20-3	Receipts	£	20-3	Payments		£
1 Jan	Balance b/d	800.50	2 Jan	A Arthur Ltd	001351	100.00
6 Jan	J Baker	495.60	9 Jan	C Curtis	001352	398.50
30 Jan	G Shotton Ltd	335.75	13 Jan	Donald & Co	001353	229.70
13 Jan	*TK Supplies BACS*	*716.50*	14 Jan	Bryant & Sons	001354	312.00
31 Jan	*Bank interest*	*5.50*	23 Jan	P Reid	001355	176.50
			23 Jan	*Omni Finance*	*DD*	*207.95*
			31 Jan	*Balance c/d*		*929.20*
		2,353.85				2,353.85
1 Feb	*Balance b/d*	*929.20*				

(b)

P GERRARD		
BANK RECONCILIATION STATEMENT AS AT 31 JANUARY 20-3		
	£	£
Closing bank statement balance		1,081.95
Less: unpresented cheques:		
Bryant & Sons (001354)	312.00	
P Reid (001355)	176.50	
		488.50
		593.45
Add: outstanding lodgement:		
G Shotton Limited		335.75
Closing cash book balance		929.20

3.5 **(a)**

Cash book (bank columns)

20-4	Receipts	£	20-4	Payments		£
1 May	Balance b/d	300	3 May	P Stone	867714	28
7 May	Cash	162	14 May	Alpha Ltd	867715	50
17 May	C Brewster	89	28 May	E Deakin	867716	110
24 May	Cash	60	17 May	Standing order: A-Z Insurance		25
28 May	Cash	40	31 May	Bank charges		10
			31 May	Balance c/d		428
		651				651
1 Jun	Balance b/d	428				

(b)

JANE DOYLE

BANK RECONCILIATION STATEMENT AS AT 31 MAY 20-4

	£
Closing bank statement balance	498
Less: unpresented cheque:	
E Deakin (867716)	110
	388
Add: outstanding lodgement:	
cash	40
Closing cash book balance	428

3.6

Statement	True	False
Unpresented cheques, outstanding lodgements and bank charges are all examples of timing differences		✓
A direct debit for car insurance of £325 is shown on the bank statement but is not entered in the cash book. This amount will need to be deducted in the bank reconciliation to make it agree with the cash book		✓
Comparing the debit side of the cash book with receipts on the bank statement will enable BACS and other automated payments missing from the cash book to be identified	✓	

3.7 **(a) – (c)**

CASH BOOK

Date	Details	Bank	Date	Cheque no	Details	Bank
20-5		£	20-5			£
1 May	Balance b/f	3,652	4 May	451762	Smith and Company	751
26 May	J Ackland	832	4 May	451763	Bryant Limited	268
28 May	Stamp Limited	1,119	7 May	451764	Curtis Cars	1,895
14 May	Perran Taxis	2,596	7 May	451765	Parts Supplies	1,045
			18 May		Wyvern Council	198
			20 May		A1 Insurance	1,005
			25 May		Okaro and Company	254
			25 May		Bank charges	20
			31 May		Balance c/d	2,763
		8,199				8,199
1 Jun	Balance b/d	2,763				

(d)

MILESTONE MOTORS

Bank Reconciliation Statement as at 31 May 20-5

	£	£
Closing bank statement balance		2,707
Less: unpresented cheque no 451764		1,895
		812
Add: outstanding lodgements:		
J Ackland	832	
Stamp Limited	1,119	
		1,951
Closing cash book balance		2,763

3.8

Cash book	Debit	Credit
	£	£
Closing balance b/d	10,341	
Adjustments:		
JC Property Co		850
Sand & Stone	2,486	
Surfrider Ltd	4,110	
Vord Finance		275
Adjusted balance c/d		15,812

Bank reconciliation	£
Closing bank statement balance	1,672
Less unpresented cheques:	
Fal Boats	760
	.
Add outstanding lodgements:	
Chiverton Ltd	1,200
Perran Ltd	4,750
P Porth	8,950
Adjusted closing cash book balance	15,812

CHAPTER 4: USE OF CONTROL ACCOUNTS

4.1   (b)   £19,100

4.2

Dr			Receivables ledger control account			Cr
20-7		£	20-7			£
1 Jun	Balance b/d	17,491	30 Jun	Sales returns		1,045
30 Jun	Sales	42,591	30 Jun	Bank		39,024
			30 Jun	Balance c/d		20,013
		60,082				60,082
1 Jul	Balance b/d	20,013				

4.3   (a)

Receivables ledger control account

Date 20-5	Details	Amount £	Date 20-5	Details	Amount £
1 Jun	Balance b/d	180,824	30 Jun	Bank	96,214
30 Jun	Sales	118,600	30 Jun	Discounts allowed	300
			30 Jun	Sales returns	650
			30 Jun	Irrecoverable debt	350
			30 Jun	Balance c/d	201,910
		299,424			299,424
1 Jul	Balance b/d	201,910			

(b)

	£
Receivables ledger control account balance as at 30 June 20-5	201,910
Total of receivables ledger accounts as at 30 June 20-5	202,260
Difference	350

(c)   The irrecoverable debt of £350 may not have been written off in the receivables ledger, and could relate to the account of Brandon Limited.

4.4 **(a)** **Receivables ledger control account**

	Amount £	Debit	Credit
Balance of credit customers at 1 September 20-2	47,238	✔	
Goods sold to credit customers	31,054	✔	
Money received from credit customers	29,179		✔
Goods returned by credit customers	2,684		✔
Discounts allowed	784		✔
Irrecoverable debt written off	450		✔

(b) (b) £45,195

(c) £467, ie £45,195 (receivables ledger control account) – £44,728 (receivables ledger)

(d) (d) and (f) are correct

4.5

	No action	Letter/email	Letter/email + phone call
Benn Ltd		✔	
Charteris & Co	✔		
D Morgan		✔	
Wilson & Sons			✔

4.6 (b) £7,400

4.7

Dr			Payables ledger control account			Cr
20-9		£	20-9			£
30 Apr	Purchases returns	653	1 Apr	Balance b/d		14,275
30 Apr	Bank	31,074	30 Apr	Purchases		36,592
30 Apr	Set-off: receivables ledger	597				
30 Apr	Balance c/d	18,543				
		50,867				50,867
			1 May	Balance b/d		18,543

4.8   **(a)**   **Payables ledger control account**

Date 20-3	Details	Amount £	Date 20-3	Details	Amount £
31 May	Bank	13,750	1 May	Balance b/d	50,300
31 May	Discounts received	500	31 May	Purchases	21,587
31 May	Purchases returns	250			
31 May	Balance c/d	57,387			
		71,887			71,887
			1 Jun	Balance b/d	57,387

(b)

	£
Payables ledger control account balance as at 31 May 20-3	57,387
Total of payables ledger accounts as at 31 May 20-3	56,387
Difference	1,000

(c)   There may have been a recording error and the debit balance of £500 for PP Properties may in fact be a credit balance.

4.9   **(a)**   **Payables ledger control account**

	Amount £	Debit	Credit
Balance of credit suppliers at 1 August 20-4	46,297		✔
Purchases from credit suppliers	22,084		✔
Payments made to credit suppliers	25,934	✔	
Discounts received	425	✔	
Goods returned to credit suppliers	1,108	✔	

(b)   (d)   £40,914

(c)

	£
Balance on payables ledger control account at 1 September 20-4	40,914
Total of the payables ledger balances at 1 September 20-4	39,906
Difference	1,008

(d) (d) A credit note was not entered in the payables ledger control account

4.10

	Debit	Credit
VAT on credit purchases	✔	
VAT on cash sales		✔
VAT on purchases returns		✔
VAT on credit sales		✔
VAT on sales returns	✔	
VAT on discounts allowed	✔	
VAT on discounts received		✔

4.11 **(a)** and **(b)**   **VAT control account**

Date 20-4	Details	Amount £	Date 20-4	Details	Amount £
30 Jun	Purchases	4,640	30 Jun	Sales	11,200
30 Jun	Sales returns	288	30 Jun	Purchases returns	224
30 Jun	Balance c/d	6,992	30 Jun	Cash sales	496
		11,920			11,920
			1 Jul	Balance b/d	6,992

(c) Is the VAT Return correct? **No**

Reason: It is likely that the VAT on sales returns has been omitted from the VAT Return. The correct amount owing to HM Revenue & Customs is £6,992.

CHAPTER 5: THE JOURNAL

5.1   (c)   Write off of a trade receivable's account from receivables ledger as an irrecoverable debt

5.2   (b)   Cash sale of goods

5.3

financial transaction	book of prime entry
• opening entries for a new business	• journal
• credit purchase of goods from a supplier	• purchases day book
• returned credit purchases to the supplier	• purchases returns day book
• customer returns goods sold on credit	• sales returns day book
• BACS receipt from a customer	• cash book
• credit sale of goods to a customer	• sales day book
• expense paid out of petty cash	• petty cash book

5.4

Date	Details	Reference	Dr	Cr
20-8			£	£
1 May	Vehicle	GL	6,500	
	Fixtures and fittings	GL	2,800	
	Inventory	GL	4,100	
	Bank	CB	150	
	Loan from husband	GL		5,000
	Capital*	GL		8,550
			13,550	13,550
	Assets and liabilities at the start of business			

*Assets – liabilities = capital (6,500 + 2,800 + 4,100 + 150 – 5,000 = 8,550)

5.5

Account name	Amount £	Debit	Credit
Cash	200	✔	
Cash at bank	2,340	✔	
Capital	9,874		✔
Trade payables	3,985		✔
Trade receivables	4,751	✔	
Loan from bank	12,650		✔
Office equipment	4,120	✔	
Rent paid	950	✔	
Inventory	2,310	✔	
Sundry expenses	1,194	✔	
Vehicles	8,350	✔	
Wages	2,294	✔	
Journal to record the opening entries of the new business			

Opening capital = £9,874 (assets £26,509 – liabilities £16,635)

5.6   (d)   Debit irrecoverable debts £240; debit VAT £48; credit receivables ledger control £288

5.7

Account name	Amount £	Debit	Credit
Irrecoverable debts	840	✔	
VAT	168	✔	
Receivables ledger control	1,008		✔

5.8   (d)   £136,035

5.9   (c)   £393,365

5.10   (a)   £240,830

5.11 **(a)** £111,650, ie £101,500 + £10,150

(b) £40,510, ie £20,500 + £9,860 + £10,150

(c) £70,290, ie £101,500 – £20,500 – £9,860 – £850

(d) **Wages expense**

Account name	Amount £	Debit	Credit
Wages expense	111,650	✔	
Wages control	111,650		✔

Liability to HM Revenue & Customs

Account name	Amount £	Debit	Credit
Wages control	40,510	✔	
HM Revenue & Customs	40,510		✔

Net wages paid to employees

Account name	Amount £	Debit	Credit
Wages control	70,290	✔	
Bank	70,290		✔

Liability for trade union fees

Account name	Amount £	Debit	Credit
Wages control	850	✔	
Trade union fees	850		✔

5.12 (a)

Account name	Amount £	Debit	Credit
Wages expense	56,110	✔	
Wages control	56,110		✔

(b)

Account name	Amount £	Debit	Credit
Wages control	21,105	✔	
HM Revenue & Customs	21,105		✔

(c)

Account name	Amount £	Debit	Credit
Wages control	32,805	✔	
Bank	32,805		✔

(d)

Account name	Amount £	Debit	Credit
Wages control	2,200	✔	
Pension fund	2,200		✔

5.13

Situation	
Harry is setting up a new business. He is starting with capital of £20,000, a vehicle valued at £8,000 and cash in the bank of £12,000.	✔
Mandy is seeking a bank loan for her business and, to impress the bank, wishes to process a journal entry for an extra £5,000 of capital which she hopes to put in at the beginning of next year.	
Tara has calculated the figures for next month's payroll. She asks if she can process the transactions through the journal.	✔
Tomasz, the bookkeeper, is going on holiday. He wants to make a journal entry of notes for the person who is covering the bookkeeping for him.	

5.14

HM Revenue & Customs			
Details	£	Details	£
Balance b/d	125	Employer's NIC	1,876
Balance c/d	5,974	Employees' NIC	1,732
		Income tax (PAYE)	2,491
	6,099		6,099

CHAPTER 6: THE TRIAL BALANCE

6.1   (b)   Purchases account

6.2   (c)   Capital account

6.3

Trial balance of Jane Greenwell as at 31 March 20-9

	Dr £	Cr £
Name of account		
Bank (overdraft)		1,250
Purchases	850	
Petty cash	48	
Sales		1,940
Purchases returns		144
Payables ledger control		1,442
Equipment	2,704	
Van	3,200	
Inventory at 1 April 20-8	1,210	
Sales returns	90	
Receivables ledger control	1,174	
Wages	1,500	
Capital		6,000
	10,776	10,776

6.4

Account name	Amount £	Debit £	Credit £
Office equipment	12,246	12,246	
Bank (cash at bank)	3,091	3,091	
Petty cash	84	84	
Inventory	11,310	11,310	
Capital	22,823		22,823
Drawings	2,550	2,550	
VAT owing to HM Revenue & Customs	3,105		3,105
Loan from bank	8,290		8,290
Payables ledger control	17,386		17,386
Receivables ledger control	30,274	30,274	
Sales	82,410		82,410
Purchases	39,496	39,496	
Purchases returns	2,216		2,216
Sales returns	3,471	3,471	
Discounts received	298		298
Discounts allowed	517	517	
Wages	20,212	20,212	
Advertising	4,390	4,390	
Insurance	1,045	1,045	
Heating and lighting	1,237	1,237	
Rent and rates	4,076	4,076	
Travel costs	854	854	
Postages	721	721	
Telephone	954	954	
Totals		136,528	136,528

6.5

Account name	Amount	Debit	Credit
	£	£	£
Sales	101,269		101,269
Sales returns	3,476	3,476	
Purchases	54,822	54,822	
Purchases returns	4,107		4,107
Receivables ledger control	25,624	25,624	
Payables ledger control	18,792		18,792
Discounts received	399		399
Discounts allowed	210	210	
Rent and rates	3,985	3,985	
Advertising	4,867	4,867	
Insurance	1,733	1,733	
Wages	31,246	31,246	
Heating and lighting	3,085	3,085	
Postages	1,211	1,211	
Telephone	985	985	
Travel costs	2,311	2,311	
Miscellaneous expenses	107	107	
Capital	22,489		22,489
Vehicles	22,400	22,400	
Inventory	12,454	12,454	
Petty cash	85	85	
Bank (overdraft)	6,291		6,291
VAT owing to HM Revenue & Customs	3,054		3,054
Loan from bank	12,200		12,200
Totals		168,601	168,601

6.6 **(a)** Bank: £3,138.58

Discounts received: £1,344.15

Receivables ledger control: £22,615.41

VAT control: £1,126.33

(b)

Item	Debit £	Credit £
Sales		61,406.53
Purchases	43,286.03	
Bank		3,138.58
Discounts received		1,344.15
Business rates	3,104.21	
Stationery	2,768.33	
Payables ledger control		4,758.39
Receivables ledger control	22,615.41	
VAT control		1,126.33
Totals	71,773.98	71,773.98

CHAPTER 7: CORRECTION OF ERRORS

7.1

Error in the general ledger	Error disclosed by the trial balance	Error not disclosed by the trial balance
A bank payment for telephone expenses has been recorded on the debit side of both the cash book and telephone expenses account	✔	
A payment recorded in bank account for vehicle repairs has been entered in vehicles account		✔
A sales invoice has been omitted from all accounting records		✔
The balance of purchases returns account has been calculated incorrectly	✔	
A bank payment from a trade receivable has been recorded in cash book and receivables ledger only	✔	
A bank payment of £85 for stationery has been recorded as £58 in both accounts		✔

7.2 (d) Error of original entry

7.3 (b) £383 debit

7.4 (a) Debit suspense account £75; credit sales account £75

7.5

Date	Details	Reference	Dr	Cr
			£	£
(a)	Business rates	GL	100	
	Rent	GL		100
(b)	Receivables ledger control	GL	96	
	Sales returns	GL		96
	Sales returns	GL	69	
	Receivables ledger control	GL		69

Date	Details	Reference	Dr	Cr
			£	£
(c)	Payables ledger control	GL	175	
	Purchases returns	GL		175
	Payables ledger control	GL	175	
	Purchases returns	GL		175
(d)	Vehicle running expenses	GL	45	
	Vehicles	GL		45

Tutorial note: Note: for errors (b) and (c) two journal entries are used. Alternatively, a single journal entry could be made for the net amount.

7.6 **(a)** Error of omission

Date	Details	Reference	Dr	Cr
			£	£
	Receivables ledger control	GL	150	
	Sales	GL		150
	Invoice no .... omitted from the accounts: in the sales ledger – debit J Rigby £150			

(b) Error of commission

Date	Details	Reference	Dr	Cr
			£	£
	Payables ledger control	GL	125	
	Payables ledger control	GL		125
	Correction of error (bank payment no ... in the payables ledger – debit H Price Limited £125 – credit H Prince £125			

(c) Error of principle

Date	Details	Reference	Dr	Cr
			£	£
	Delivery van	GL	10,000	
	Vehicle expenses	GL		10,000
	Correction of error – vehicle no .... invoice no .... debited to vehicle expenses in error			

(d) Reversal of entries

Date	Details	Reference	Dr	Cr
			£	£
	Postages	GL	55	
	Bank	CB		55
	Removing the incorrect entry: bank payment on ...(date)... for postages entered on the wrong side of both accounts			

Date	Details	Reference	Dr	Cr
			£	£
	Postages	GL	55	
	Bank	CB		55
	Recording the correct entry: bank payment on ...(date)... for postages entered on the wrong side of both accounts			

(e) Compensating error

Date	Details	Reference	Dr	Cr
			£	£
	Purchases	GL	100	
	Purchases returns	GL		100
	Correction of undercast on purchases account and purchases returns account on ...(date)...			

(f) Error of original entry

Date	Details	Reference	Dr	Cr
			£	£
	Receivables ledger control	GL	98	
	Bank	CB		98
	Removing the incorrect entry: bank receipt for £89 on ...(date)... recorded as £98 instead of £89; in the receivables ledger debit L Johnson £98			

Date	Details	Reference	Dr	Cr
			£	£
	Bank	CB	89	
	Receivables ledger control	GL		89
	Recording the correct entry: bank receipt for £89 on ...(date)... recorded as £98 instead of £89; in the receivables ledger credit L Johnson £89			

7.7

Telephone expenses account

Details	Amount £	Details	Amount £
Suspense	210		

Suspense account

Details	Amount £	Details	Amount £
Balance b/f	110	Telephone expenses	210
Sales	100		

Sales account

Details	Amount £	Details	Amount £
		Suspense	100

Vehicle expenses account

Details	Amount £	Details	Amount £
Vehicles	50		

Vehicles account

Details	Amount £	Details	Amount £
		Vehicle expenses	50

7.8 **(a)** **(1)**

Account name	Amount £	Debit	Credit
Value Added Tax	700	✔	

(2)

Account name	Amount £	Debit	Credit
Value Added Tax	800		✔

(3)

Account name	Amount £	Debit	Credit
Suspense	100	✔	

(b) **(1)**

Account name	Amount £	Debit	Credit
Bank	98	✔	
Vehicle expenses	98		✔

(2)

Account name	Amount £	Debit	Credit
Vehicle expenses	89	✔	
Bank	89		✔

7.9

Date	Details	Reference	Dr	Cr
			£	£
(a)	Office expenses	GL	85	
	Suspense	GL		85
	Omission of entry in office expenses account – bank payment made on ....(date)....			
(b)	Suspense	GL	78	
	Photocopying	GL		78
	Removing the incorrect entry: bank payment for photocopying £87 entered in photocopying account as £78 in error			
	Photocopying	GL	87	
	Suspense	GL		87
	Recording the correct entry: bank payment for photocopying £87 entered in photocopying account as £78 in error			
(c)	Suspense	GL	100	
	Sales returns	GL		100
	Overcast on ...(date)... now corrected			
(d)	Commission received	GL	25	
	Suspense	GL		25
	Commission received on ....(date) entered twice in commission received account, now corrected			

Note: for error (b) a single entry can be made for the net amount.

Dr			Suspense account		Cr
20-4		£	20-4		£
30 Sep	Trial balance difference	19	(a)	Office expenses	85
(b)	Photocopying	78	(b)	Photocopying	87
(c)	Sales returns	100	(d)	Commission received	25
		――			――
		197			197
		――			――

7.10

Account names	Balances on 31 December 20-4	Balances at 2 January 20-5	
	£	Debit £	Credit £
Office equipment	12,246	12,246	
Bank (cash at bank)	3,091	3,091	
Petty cash	84	84	
Inventory	11,310	11,310	
Capital	18,246		18,246
Loan from bank	8,290		8,290
VAT owing to HM Revenue & Customs	3,105		3,105
Payables ledger control	17,386		17,386
Receivables ledger control	30,274	30,274	
Sales	82,410		82,410
Purchases	39,996	*39,496*	
Purchases returns	2,216		2,216
Sales returns	3,471	3,471	
Wages	20,212	20,212	
Advertising	4,300	*4,390*	
Insurance	1,045	1,045	
Heating and lighting	1,237	1,237	
Rent and business rates	4,076	4,076	
Postages	721	721	
Suspense account (credit balance)	410		–
Totals		131,653	131,653

Tutorial note: the accounts affected by the journal entries are purchases, advertising and suspense.

7.11

Account names	Balances on 30 April 20-8	Balances at 1 May 20-8	
	£	Debit £	Credit £
Sales	101,169		*101,269*
Sales returns	3,476	3,476	
Purchases	54,822	54,822	
Purchases returns	4,107		4,107
Receivables ledger control	25,624	25,624	
Payables ledger control	18,792		18,792
Rent and rates	3,985	3,985	
Advertising	4,867	4,867	
Insurance	1,733	1,733	
Wages	27,391	*31,246*	
Heating and lighting	3,085	3,085	
Miscellaneous expenses	107	107	
Capital	18,171		18,171
Vehicles	22,400	22,400	
Inventory	12,454	12,454	
Petty cash	85	85	
Bank (overdraft)	6,041		*6,291*
VAT owing to HM Revenue & Customs	3,054		3,054
Loan from bank	12,200		12,200
Suspense account (debit balance)	3,505	–	
Totals		163,884	163,884

Tutorial note: the accounts affected by the journal entries are sales, wages, bank and suspense.

7.12 **(a)**

Statement	
A suspense account is created when errors are not disclosed by the trial balance.	
A suspense account can have either a debit balance or a credit balance.	✔
When the debit side total of a trial balance is less than the credit side total, a suspense is opened with a debit balance.	✔
If the errors cannot be found quickly, the balance of suspense account is written off to irrecoverable debts account.	

(b)

Error	Disclosed	Not disclosed
Purchases account has been undercast by £1,000.	✔	
Amy used personal cash to pay for fuel for the business van but has forgotten to record the transaction in the accounts.		✔

7.13 **(a)**

£ 1,516

Debit	✓
Credit	

(b)

30 June 20-2			Journal number 49
Account	**Debit**	**Credit**	**Description**
	£	**£**	
Rent paid	1,525		Correction of error 1
Suspense		1,525	Correction of error 1
Suspense	9		Correction of error 2
Sales		9	Correction of error 2

Tutorial note: the difference of £9 has been entered here. An alternative treatment is to take out the wrong figure of £1,445 (debit sales; credit suspense) and then record the correct figure of £1,454 (debit suspense; credit sales). The effect is the same as the net amount of £9 shown above.

7.14

Item	Debit £	Credit £
Sales		82,813.50
Purchases	52,894.68	
Discounts allowed	282.48	
Bank	10,886.27	
Vehicles	33,610.34	
Payables ledger control		14,860.27
Totals	97,673.77	97,673.77

Index

for your notes

for your notes

for your notes

for your notes

for your notes

for your notes